Generation Z

A Guide To Understand And Educate
Gen Z Students

*(The Complete Manual To Understand Lead
The Next Generation)*

Richard Walls

Published By **Zoe Lawson**

Richard Walls

All Rights Reserved

Generation Z: A Guide To Understand And Educate Gen Z Students (The Complete Manual To Understand Lead The Next Generation)

ISBN 978-1-77485-597-3

No part of this guidebook shall be reproduced in any form without permission in writing from the publisher except in the case of brief quotations embodied in critical articles or reviews.

Legal & Disclaimer

The information contained in this ebook is not designed to replace or take the place of any form of medicine or professional medical advice. The information in this ebook has been provided for educational & entertainment purposes only.

The information contained in this book has been compiled from sources deemed reliable, and it is accurate to the best of the Author's knowledge; however, the Author cannot guarantee its accuracy and validity and cannot be held liable for any errors or omissions. Changes are periodically made to this book. You must consult your doctor or get professional medical advice before using any of the suggested remedies, techniques, or information in this book.

Upon using the information contained in this book, you agree to hold harmless the Author from and against any damages, costs, and expenses, including any legal fees potentially resulting from the application of any of the information provided by this guide. This disclaimer applies to any damages or injury caused by the use and application, whether directly or indirectly, of any advice or information presented, whether for breach of contract, tort, negligence, personal injury, criminal intent, or under any other cause of action.

You agree to accept all risks of using the information presented inside this book. You need to consult a professional medical practitioner in order to ensure you are both able and healthy enough to participate in this program.

Table of contents

Introduction 1

Chapter 1: Who Is Generation Z? 4

Chapter 2: Examining The Motivations Behind Generation Z's Unique Approach To Finance 11

Chapter 3: What Can You Create Wealth That Is Real As Gen Zer? 4 Steps To Get You On The Right Track 21

Chapter 4: Tips For Marketing For The Gen Z Guy/Girl To Further Improve Their Financial Vehicles 38

Chapter 5: How To Know Generation Z .. 54

Chapter 6: Understanding Their Behaviors 60

Chapter 7: The Traits That Are Associated With Adulthood 71

Chapter 8: Teaching The Next Generation 85

Chapter 9: Providing Guidance To Students In Career Options 94

Chapter 10: Gen Z And Social Problems 101

Chapter 11: Learn To Be Aware Of The Stoic In You 107

Chapter 12: Uncover The Meaning Of Stoicism 114

Chapter 13: Learn What Passion Is....... 127

Chapter 14: Achieve Freedom From Passion.. 137

Chapter 15: Be Aware Of Your Stoic Virtues And Emotions 150

Chapter 16: Generation Z On Time Management 159

Conclusion 184

Introduction

Every generation has their own way of looking at finance and money. For instance, millennials discovered that the path to adulthood was filled with all kinds of challenges... There was stagnant wage growth, unpredictability in economic conditions and more. These issues as well as other circumstances and experiences of generations have shaped the financial outlook of this generation and behavior. The millennials grew up prepared to take whatever risk was necessary to lift out of the slow-moving financial sludge they grew up in. In particular, they turned the tame and financially uninformed internet environment into a lucrative multi-billion-dollar industry.

You're not like the typical generation of millennials. And the differences are obvious.

As a Gen Zer you probably grew up in the in the middle of a recession (unless it's the case that you're part of the youngest generation in the Generation Zers.). Like the millennials, your parents did not let you grow up a victim to (tame) consequences of a stagnant and boring economic system... Your parents raised you from the rubble and ashes of a depressed economy.

You might not have realized that but it happened. The recession probably affected you in one way or other. Maybe you thought of a toy you wanted in your the back of your head however your parents weren't able to purchase it for you. Perhaps they had a reason for why they couldn't because the global economy was in turmoil... People lost their jobs (and life) all over the place, and right all over. Dad and mom, as a result were required to be cautious of what they spent to buy, but you were forced to choose a less expensive toy.

Growing up with this in your background has had an impact on you. Perhaps some of your older peers believe you're too strict. They might think you'd rather cling to the things you've got instead of being imaginative... as the youngster of your age. They should be able to see that you're merely prudent; you've experienced things as a child and didn't enjoy these things. It's not that you'd prefer to not have fun and live your life in the present; you would like to, and desperately...

But more than anything, you'd rather not have to settle for less because you didn't have enough money or you faced as a child.

It examines how to understand the Gen Z mindset toward finance. It will analyze the psychology of Gen Zers, the many positive financial habits and other aspects. It will also perform "open-brain operation" and show you how you can see things in a certain way and also why you'd prefer not take certain actions. It will let you know that there are millions with the same issues as you. It will also help you ensure your financial security, from now on, to ensure that you don't need to worry about money.

Chapter 1: Who Is Generation Z?

Generation Z is the generation that was born between 1996 to 2014. You can add or subtract years at both ends.

There are the 82 million Generation Zers. Generation Z (largely) arrived at their twenties right in the midst of an economic downturn. With the oldest of this generation entering the 21st century next year (2019)and the most senior is just about to enter the workforce and you're likely familiar with the rules and regulations of financial matters in your unique manner. It is based on any personal experiences you've experienced, due to your parent(s) growing up right into the center of a recession. It might be that you had to be raised without certain things or you were forced relocate to a smaller home in a less desirable area the town... and your mother or dad attempted to convince you to you that it was a difficult time. However, you didn't know the way that things had changed in a flash.

You along with you and the Digital World: A Unique Relationship

Older generations, as well as who played leading roles in the field of digital technology, be in admiration for what technology has brought to the table.

On your other hand, might be just nonchalant about it. Why? Because you have grown up in the age of technology. It's hard to think of the last time you didn't have smartphones, tablets... and any kind of screen you could use a swipe on. It's commonplace for you and the rest of your friends to know that a couple of swipes on a mobile screen can get you accomplished. Why should you be amazed by something that is so well-known to you? If someone dropped an old model tape player from the 80s and you were awestruck, you'd be. This is not just for show. If someone is trying to impress you with their most recent iPhone model, well... the chances are likely than not you already own one or plan to purchase one in the near future.

It's not about the cool devices that have been a part of your life, you're unique from generations of people:

You and your fellow young'uns Already Earning Money...

According to research according to studies, 77 percent from those in the Gen Z demographic is already making and spending their own money. Do you feel like this personally? It's likely. Perhaps you've completed some work and made some money during the process? Maybe you've supervised some of your neighbors, or created an flier for your elderly family member? If not, there are likely to be others who have accomplished it. There are a myriad of ways to earn money as Gen Zer such as running an infant-sitting service, assisted by your peers or make affiliate sales through eBay or give music lessons, take on a part-time position and freelance work and even earn some money from dad and mom and so on.

In short, Gen Zers- your generation - earn and spend money at their own pace.

There's more .....

You are cautious about risk, and are Flexible

Experiences as a Gen Zer have greatly shaped you into the person you are today. Particularly, as a Generation Zer, you may have discovered long back that things could alter rapidly, and within a few minutes. We've given several abstract instances... Some of them, like your younger self witnessing neighbors lose their homes or seeing your parents relocate to a smaller, more shabby home - could be particularly near home even if you don't intend it that way. This is one reason that many Gen Z consumers - not only you - are conscious of their spending habits. This is why you're so eager to record your purchases, regardless of your older friends attempts to convince that you "let your hair down and have fun with your youth."

There's a term that's known as "buyer's regret" "... maybe you've heard of it? It's when a buyer feels regret following a purchase when they realize that in the end, they just wanted the item but do not really need it. Have you ever purchased something but then feel regret for having "wasted the money"? It's not uncommon The buyer's remorse afflicts the majority of Gen Zers. They are able to change and discover ways to achieve objectives without spending real money. For instance you could opt to rent items; utilize the items for the entire rental period, then consider whether buying a product makes sense. Have you ever rented a game prior to purchasing it to determine if it's worth the cost? Yes? You're not unusual or uncooperative for doing this. A lot of people in your age range did it. It's just a matter of wiring your brain.

Do you and the other Gen Zers see yourself to be "Digital natives"?

We may be incorrect, but the truth is not. Do you think you are digital native? Many of your peers laugh at the term. Many Gen Zers, are today's children that are between 5 and 6 years old playing with iPads and iPhones and other devices that fit the term "digital native" better. Does this sound like you? It's very likely that it does.

Many Gen Zers were witness to the explosion of the Internet bubble even though you might be too young to fully comprehend the intricate nature of. It was your turn to be "humanized" enough by this , in a manner that those who are post-Gen Z likely never will ever be. So, even though our 6-year-olds may truly think that they do not really require interaction in the real world and that the web/virtual world is far more than enough for them, it's difficult to prove this claim to you.

It's because you've been there. You've been there as a young person, when family members and neighbors lost their homes in a single day and needed to relocate cross-state. You've experienced it. So, you're already human in a way that your generation's next generation isn't. That's a good aspect for you.

You have a love-hate relation with money

Money is an instrument... is it is it? It allows you to live your life with freedom and autonomy, is it not? In the same way... an absence of cash could mean you losing your freedom and independence regardless of the meaning in your life. This is a perfectly reasonable idea. You are aware that the loss of money can be catastrophic the financial situation, and you're right.

You (likely) are taking a mature attitude towards the possibility of failure

What research researchers say about you:

Gen Z believe that moments of failure can be an chance to attempt and try again... repeatedly. The majority of Gen Zers believe that they will encounter significant failures before they achieve success.

Do you feel like the following... in your school, home, at the field, or the rink? ...? Most likely, you could.

Let's continue with the discussion, where we'll concentrate on Gen Zers approach to financing.

Chapter 2: Examining The Motivations Behind Generation Z's Unique Approach To Finance

This chapter will build on the preceding one.

So far, you're already aware of financial events and other elements which may have shaped your outlook as Gen Zer. This chapter aims to provide an accurate understanding of the same.

Why is it crucial to learn about the thrifty and risk-averse mindset to life of your Gen Zer colleagues?

Why not study the shrewd tough and simple actions plans that you are so comfortable with?

Why is it crucial to comprehend your (collective) perspective even if you already recognize what you're made of? Why?

This is because you'll no longer feel like you're a different person. It's possible to feel like you're living your life in a way that isn't right, at the very least, compared the accounts of your parents or older acquaintances' stories in their personal accounts.

You can accept both your personal and financial flaws once you are aware of your mentality. There's nothing wrong with worrying about financial stability... thousands of your friends have to worry about it all the time as you do. You're no misfit. You're as regular and normal as you can get.

There will be numerous comparisons between Gen Zers and millennials both in this chapter as well as the prior ones. These are important to assess your thinking and help you to make multiple points. There are few things that provide as potent as a set of tools for learning as comparison and contrast.

There are many references to millennials are found here; do not look down on them.

And what better way to examine Gen Z's mindset than to examine Gen Z mindset, than to switch into story-mode and then look at a possible Gen Z example:

It's a cool afternoon in late summer within Tacoma, WA. Maya Cyrus, 19 years old, is just beginning her second year of university in

Puget Sound University. She's 19 so this puts her in the middle in Gen Z.

As with most of her classmates; Maya does not view university as a space for leisure, navel-gazing or self-discovery. The recession came to an end when she was just 10 years old. older. It was still a child when she went through it however, she was capable of comprehending the issues and following the simplified explanations provided from her parents. The experiences she experienced and also watching from afar have affected her approach to life. The higher education system is not an exception.

Maya is already thinking about her life after college. In fact she's been thinking about this since she first began her time at Puget Sound. She admits that there's plenty of pressure in securing an employment after college and sustaining yourself. Instead of soaking up university life, squeeze the most enjoyment from it, and drag the time as long possible, she's focused to whittle away her four years of college as fast as she can and then launching the "good career direction." As she says, and other of her colleagues it's harder to reflect since there's always the worry of how you'll be capable to survive in the current economy in the event that "you don't have a clear direction."

Companies have (very appropriately) started paying the attention of Gen Z

In recent times the millennial generation has been the subject of the media's attention. In fact, they are the most studied demographic in the history of mankind. However, the moment the (and the Maya's) generation grows older and is preparing to enter the workforce, companies are paying attention even more.

Gen Z Gen Z, as we've already mentioned is 82 million strong. That means that you have a higher percentage of Generation X by at least 7 million. It's not difficult to be labelled "millennials... but with more time wasted on social mediaand and too lazy to go about buying other than online but with a nicer collaboration and a more sociable nature."

However, you're aware that this actually not the case. Even to the older generation the last sentence will show that you're significantly more than "a technology-savvy, internet-savvy version of the millennials." Generation

Zers have been raised in a completely different historical environment' than the millennials. This has provided you with an unique perspective of the world different from everyone other.

Pioneers versus... not-pioneers: Millennials versus Gen Zers

The millennials are the internet pioneers. They invented websites like Facebook. They introduced the concept of purchasing items using their phones as well as the transition from satellite television and satellite TV to Netflix along with Hulu.

It is evident that their journey is filled with shifts... this is logical considering that they were the pioneers. On however, are unable to recall your life in the absence of those 21st Century life "basics." Shopping with your mobile isn't likely to inspire much excitement in your... You've been doing it since you learned the concept that is "shopping."

The millennial generation changed the world in significant ways; they helped elect the first president of African descent in the history of our country and led to mass education of racial issues and to legalize gay weddings. The other hand, consider these events as normal. It's true that the generation of millennials coincided with a huge economic boom and the people who bought numerous houses as if they was the most common thing to do. They were shocked by an employment market that was less welcoming and a bit less appealing following their departure from college. On contrary were shaped in one way or another by the economic downturn. Your peers and you are conditioned and ready to put in the effort to make an enduring future for yourself in a manner that millennials weren't.

The early responsibility, maturity and continuous monetary awareness

Returning to our hypothetical case: Maya Cyrus is fairly typical (to all of the previously mentioned) in this way. Although she experienced the economic downturn at an early age however, she was raised in a "solidly middle-class" home in California. Her father earned a decent salary as a professor and her mother earned a decent income from her artistic career. She is however aware that money is an unpredictable client.

Are there parallels to your own life? Maybe you see a number of similarities?

At 19 as Maya Gen Zers are responsible, mature and financially aware than their parents would ever imagine being at the same age.

In her situation, Maya's first step, when she was able to take on an internship for the magazine of college alumni to help pay the costs. While she's aware that her parents won't be spending a lot of money on tuition but she's always aware of the expense that her schooling will cost her. Maya has thought about having a gap year for the sake of being able to have a'real life' other than being a responsible and accountable student.'

However, she's not keen on that, after having done some thought-provoking. If you get off the treadmill for just a few minutes, you'll begin accruing the interest you owe on student loans' in addition to other things. She'd prefer not to pay unnecessary charges on her loans, in addition to other things', and, as such, is deciding against the option of a gap-year. This is a thought-process you might share, all the way down to the most basic.

Perhaps you've seen certain of your old pals carry huge amounts of debt during their school years and purchasing items they believed were essential. It is also possible to have watched their struggle to find decent paying jobs that would suit their talents. These kinds of things tend to create a lasting impression.

This is why you and a lot of your friends have adopted an approach that is much more practical to your personal finances. Many parents believe that Gen Zers are more likely to jump in headfirst into new technologies and risky financial choices, similar to the millennials did before them. However, many Gen Zers did not have the security of a booming, affluence-drenched economy, as the millennials did.

It is possible that you want to most importantly, get lucrative jobs that pay well when you get old enough. You'd prefer to preserve your savings instead of spending money you don't have. When you don't have cash, you should to pursue it actively with the avenues and channels established by the naturally creative generation of millennials.

Work and school... how Gen Z does it. method

In this particular chapter, and what you could easily identify as Gen Zer All kinds of educational experiences are seen as a way to achieve a financial goal. That's right... college is an opportunity to create solid skills which employers will value. This can, in turn, assure a long-lasting career.

This is why eighty percent of first Gen Z grad class (in 2017) and one that you might have been a part of (if your birth year was 1996) chose their fields with job-related opportunities in mind.

The world was far since the time when many college students were willing to choose art programs that offered little in the way of a huge improvement in terms of future employment opportunities.

Furthermore, the majority of Gen Z grads are more than ready to step out of their comfort zones and do the hard work. For example:

75% of them are willing to relocate to another state , if a convincing job opportunity comes up.

* 58% of employees are willing to work evenings or even on weekends.

* 78% have since completed an internship/apprenticeship

77% earn additional income through the freelance market, such as part-time work as well as earned compensation (there are chapters devoted to this in the book)

35% of them have their own companies or are currently in the process of setting up one soon (there are chapters devoted to this topic in the book)

Now, you know how you might be so'severe in your approach to finances. You may have been curious all your life you to know why you saw spending and finance in the way you do... then here it is. It's not that you're not looking forward to living your life... It's that you'd prefer to be financially secure first to start off from. It's a good thing.

The next step is to discuss steps that Gen Z folks can use to create wealth and financial independence.

Chapter 3: What Can You Create Wealth That Is Real As Gen Zer? 4 Steps To Get You On The Right Track

There may be ambitions and desires to become millionaire. As Gen Zers may not have the luxury of big pay checks and generous bonuses that could make you reach millionaire status. This is okay... you're blessed with the most powerful resource available to you the time.

Being a millionaire doesn't need to mean huge salaries as well as the trappings that come with the. The best method to earn millions (or millions) in particular for Gen Zers is to keep growing your earnings. You save it, put it into investments it, and plan your budget to live on less than what you earn.

These are actions you can take being a Gen Zer which can almost assure you of a wealth-building experience.

Step #1: Whatever Earnings You Earn, Save A Percentage and let it compound

It is best to start with the simplest techniques... such as keeping track of your savings.

As you enter your twenties and teens It is important to save to the maximum extent you can and to do it regularly too. One of your strengths is that you're not entrusted with the kind of responsibility as older adults have to take on. Therefore, you should aim to save at minimum 20% of the earnings. You can even automatize your savings to ensure you can ensure that 20% of each pay check is automatically taken and put aside.

The next chapter will provide the most practical, easy avenues you can pursue to earn an income as Gen Zer.

Saving money when you're young is essential. You can make your money compound for a longer period of time and therefore gain more benefits than many people are able to. The compound interest can be your best friend, especially when you're an aspiring young person. A few decades later you'll be amazed the extent to which you've been able to build your savings.

Step 2: Be Goal-Oriented

This is the time to think about identification of your goals, quantifying them, and prioritizing the pursuit of the goals you want to achieve. The earlier you can get into it the better it'll be for you.

Establish a solid base. You'll be able to achieve this by mastering cash flow. How can one master the flow of cash when you are your older age? You do it in the traditional way by digging in to the information, studying carefully, watching relevant videos etc. Also, you examine your lifestyle and habits of spending.

What did you spend your money onin the last twelve months? What are you able to save over time? Determine what a comfortable and real-life style is for you.

We'll use a millennial case to highlight a few of the points however, please don't ignore this. He is only a half-decade older than the Gen Zers with the longest lifespan. Brandon Copeland is an NFL player. He is 26, and he can save almost 100 percent of his earnings. He states that "saving is not dependent on the amount you earn, it's all about the way you spend your money."

When you have a record of your expenses, you are able to begin to save in earnest. This will assist you in figuring out what you'll need to eliminate.

As you're a Gen Zer You are in the point where your expenditures are never going to be lower. Even if you haven't yet gotten to the point where the real money starts coming in even though you're still living a life of a college student (this happens in your 20s) it's the perfect time as any to lay a strong financial base.

Step 3: Don't be a Lifestyle Cruser; Do Your Best to Live Below Your Expectations

As Gen Zer You may be in the same way as your peers and what trends they follow. You might be looking for modern technology, frequent traveling, fashionable clothes, etc.

There's nothing wrong in this. But it can become problematic when you're not able to save any money since you're spending excessively. Control how much you are spending. Be careful with your spending. If you're clever (and you are since you're Gen Zer) then you'll enjoy an active, happy life, while taking important financial decisions.

Step 4: Foundation the Foundation, the Foundation

It's not too late an opportunity to lay your foundation. In fact, it's an ideal time. Concentrate on achieving such immediate goals like cash reserves. You can make your regular purchases, and save to the extent you can.

You can also invest in investment. Your parents can assist you to take your first steps in the investment industry. This chapter is going to address this and provide you with specific avenues you can join. The objective is to create an established financial foundation, in order to leverage this in the near future, to create real wealth.

You probably already know whom Warren Buffett is. He is among the world's richest men. Yes, it's true that he made the majority of his current fortune after he reached the age of 55. What doesn't get enough coverage is that the sole reason that this particular scenario was possible was because he was so meticulous with money during his teens and early 20s. He created a variety of income sources as streams, channels, and streams in his early years. The growth, over the years, resulted in at age 55, he'd earned lots lots of cash through the reserves he put down when he was a child.

Warren Buffett is a perfect model of Gen Zers. In fact, he had a generation of Gen Zers long before Gen Z was a thing.

Next chapter is going to focus on the ways and methods you can earn money as Gen Zer. They'll be simple, practical avenues to use to "flex" your knowledge to the maximum extent possible without fearing that you'll slip up and making mistakes which can cause you to be in trouble for the long haul.

How Do You Earn Money As a Gen Z Girl or Guy? Easy, low-maintenance cash options for Generation Z

Of all the methods to earn cash, Gen Z has been the most focused on making money through online ventures. This may be easy to grasp that not only are transportation expenses almost nonexistent, the access to information is readily available and the variety of skills that can be utilized is endless;

Generation Zers have grown up knowing the web.

You probably began using phones and tablets from the age of a child and your primary source for information was the internet. Furthermore it is the only place that provides so many possibilities for technical, and even professional expressions for Gen Zers - most of whom are not old enough to fully absorbed into traditional financial avenues and systems, like the internet. This is perhaps the reason why there are teens with millions of users on the YouTube channel, as well as millions of dollars in their names,. You may have even signed up to a few. The majority of options and methods to earn money involve a lot using the internet.

Here are tried and tested strategies for Gen Zers to earn money.

1. Redeem money when you purchase online items

This is a great option for those who frequent online shopping. Many websites permit you to receive your money back. You must know what they are , and then change your purchasing habits to ensure you are able to use these sites. One of the best is Ebates.com and has a partnership and with online retailers. It is a simple user-friendly app. A purchase can earn you anything from 6-12 percent of the purchase amount back. Each quarter, this website will give you the entire cash back via an PayPal payment or through a checks.

Effectively, you earn money to shop. It's a fantastic way to earn passive money.

2. Be Strenuous With the Surveys

1. Take surveys that are simple.

Participating in surveys is one of the most simple and quickest ways to earn money on the internet. In just a few seconds, you could earn a few dollars with a couple of clicks and answering a couple of (often common) questions.

A site such as SwagBucks provides a variety of simple questionnaires that you can complete within a few minutes. Earn points rather than directly earning dollars, but you can convert these points into actual dollars that are mailed into your PayPal accounts.

If you're a Gen Zer and is able to spend a couple of hours each day on the commute, why not make use of this time to earn couple of dollars? All you require is only a few minutes of survey time... you can build up to 20 surveys in a short time If you're consistent your earnings will build to a significant cash-flow.

Here are similar sites that allow you to make money via surveys: InboxDollars.com, Prize Rebel, GlobalTestMarket.Com, Vindale.com and PineconeResearch.Com

I. Talk about entertainment and shopping

If we're discussing ways to earn money and surveys are an effective way to this end, it's not logical to not make surveys on such fun aspects of life like shopping and entertainment.

In a world that is becoming increasingly consumer-oriented increasingly, people require the help of a "spotter" who can tell them whether item is X or Y offers worth to money.

Websites such as Nielsen Computer and Mobile Panel have a myriad of surveys specifically focused on media, travel shopping, entertainment, and preferences. If you're Gen Z and like the idea of being money to critique your favourite TV series, there are several platforms that can help you achieve this.

Iii. Let us know your opinion

Gen Zers (and more to an extent, the millennials) are often criticized as being snowflakes who are special. In a way they really are due to the fact that they've been sheltered by their parents throughout their childhood. But, they have developed enough individualism to that you have a good possibility of earning money by sharing your opinions.

There are websites for survey like Survey Junkie that exclusively ask to hear your opinions on items. It doesn't matter what is your favorite food item, TV show or shampoo you love your thoughts can be very helpful in telling companies what people would like to hear and what they don't like about their products.

3. Grow your savings

i. Use the automatic savings feature.

Gen Zers have a lot of luck, and do not need to be reminded by them to understand why financial planning is crucial. Many Gen Zers are aware of the importance of having a responsible budget and saving money, focusing on the lowest priced items, etc. The majority of Gen Zers had to deal with the effects of the economic downturn while young and highly inquisitive. So, the issue of financial planning isn't necessarily as tense like it can be when millennials are involved.

Anyone is able to open a bank account today. It is possible that you will need the support of a parent in case you are not yet an adult However there are many special programs specifically designed for those who are under 18.

If you choose to use any of the options to earn money discussed in this chapter, the amount of money you earn will automatically transferred into an account for savings.

4. Place your money in a savings account

iinvest in items that are important to you.

The first thing to do is probably already have millions of things that appeal to you and that you might want to put your money into. As Gen Zers you are still at an age that you might not have the same financial knowledge as those who are older. However, this shouldn't be an issue. The application Stash is an excellent investment tool.

The design is straightforward while the needs are modest. The minimum requirement for your initial investment is $500. The concept here is to learn as you go and, as time passes as you input information on your desires and interests, the app will lead you to investments which match your needs. The investment breakdowns are clear as well as real investment teams.

II. You can invest in the stock market using your phone

Being a GenZer you'll become extremely proficient in investing in stocks at the age of 30 If you continue to work at it. In the present it is, you must follow the necessary baby steps to ensure that you will only make mistakes that are necessary and losses that do not destroy your enthusiasm.

If you're looking to getting started with the stock market, websites such as Robinhood can help you get into the market for free.

Here are some other options for stock market investing apps that are perfect to your needs: Acorns.com, Stockpile.com, E*Trade Mobile, Charles Schwab & TradeHero

5: Play games & binge-watch videos

I- Play games on your savings account

Apps like The Long Game app are an exciting method of Gen Zers to earn money and have fun while doing it. The app itself is an ordinary savings account but it also comes with exciting features, such as games. You can play games available and earn rewards in bitcoin or cash.

The more you save the more chances to win. There is also a possibility of winning prizes at least $1 million. This is a incredible savings account, no matter what. It's also ideal for Gen Zers.

II. Sell your gold

Are you into gaming? Do you love playing games such as FIFA Ultimate Team 19,

Pokemon Go and Overwatch? Then you must think about selling your characters, gold equipment, as well as rare items at auctions of players for actual cash.

There are always players trying to get better by using shortcuts that involves using real money to purchase features for games. Particularly, if you have uncommon characters or a few spruced-up gems, you can make some decent money.

iii- Watch videos

It's a fact. You could (and can) earn money for watching online videos. Apps like MyPoints let you do online shopping, view videos, read emails and even take surveys to earn points. When you've earned enough points, you can be reimbursed via gifts cards, or PayPal money. In addition, you'll get an instant cash injection of $5 for the first five surveys you complete.

6: Work online alone

Graphic design gigs

Do you have any experience with graphic design? Are you a fan of graphic design, and maybe self-styled? If so, you could earn money through designing as a freelancer... And you'll earn money doing something you love.

For instance, 99Designs can let you practice your design skills by creating designs for book covers and magazine covers. Also, you'll be able to design for companies that are who require attractive illustrations or business cards.

Another great benefit is that you can determine your availability and cost. This means that, unless you would like to, you will not be required to stay up all night or finish work during the weekend.

ii- Audio transcription

Audio transcription is a well-known method of earning extra money for Gen Zers because all it takes is listening to recordings of audio and recording what you hear. Websites such as TranscribeMe! and Tigerfish provide quick, efficient transcription jobs that are available to everyone.

If you are fluent in another language, you could offer translation services on these sites and earn well.

iii- Translate documents

The majority of translation jobs include obtaining work and later translating them into different languages, making them available to different publics.

If you have multiple languages in your repertoire or know a language of a rarer variety and you can earn even more income. These websites like Gengo, VerbalizeIt, and Rev have a wide range of translation possibilities provided you have the abilities.

7: Earn money online

I-Blog at home

Blogging can be a blessing especially for Gen Zers. It certainly is. You are able to be at your own pace. You can write from anywhere and write about everything.

Particularly as a Gen Zer and with a lot of your peers logging many hours online, you could make thousands of dollars through blogging. It's not an exaggeration. In reality, there are teenagers who make six figures in a month through blogging and other related activities.

At first you'll not earn many dollars. It is possible to spend months without making one cent. If you continue to do it, followers (and money) will begin to come. It's not unusual for bloggers to say that they earned "around thirty thousand dollars this month".

I. Start with your YouTube Channel.

This is a top choice for Gen Zers. All you need is the smartphone camera and adequate lighting to start. If you are able, purchasing a tripod would make sense as it gives you to have more energy and hands-off activities. It is possible to earn a significant amount of money by operating an YouTube channel. All you have to do is create relevant content and keep the atmosphere fun. Similar to blog posts, it is possible to earn several thousand dollars each month through the production of interesting videos on YouTube.

The next step is to discuss marketing strategies for Gen Zers.

Chapter 4: Tips For Marketing For The Gen Z Guy/Girl To Further Improve Their Financial Vehicles

If you are starting your own company it will be more successful when you can attract people. To entice people to the point that they will follow your content and be patiently waiting for the next update It will allow you to become an effective marketer. In addition, it will assist in being a more effective marketer to the Gen Zers. What is the reason? The reason is that your content is likely to be targeted to the Gen Z crowd who will make up the largest portion of your target audience.

Here are some suggestions to help you make it through to this often anxious demographic:

1. Rather than creating ads, you should make value

Many people complained that millennials do not have a lot of a filter to promote content. Actually they continue to make a fuss about it. However, millennials are just youngsters playing, in comparison with Gen Zers.

Gen Zers did not have to contend with CDMA or EDGE connections. The millennials did, therefore they're more willing to use a little perseverance and settle for a bit longer before they can access their favorite content. Generation Zers have gotten used to fast internet connections and easy access to the internet from the moment they first became familiar online. They prefer to cut to the point, using very little marketing. What you won't get with if you have many ads and lots of promotions to your content is being overlooked by an alternative who has similar content.

2. Observing the character is essential.

If your site is unfinished and appears to be built 12 years ago using Python it will appear aged and outdated regardless of how old you are and how well-crafted your content is.

Gen Zers don't wish to hear about the level of expert you are. They evaluate things with the eyes. A professional, neatly-designed layout with a green screen can earn you lots of praise from Gen Zers and they will be more attracted by what you can provide.

3. They don't focus on what you are selling, they are more interested in how you can assist them.

Gen Z is aware of the potential of the internet and technological advancements. In fact, a lot of Gen Zers consider being an online influencer as a significant a choice for a career as getting an engineering degree. They're not "reaching" in the same way They've witnessed numerous of their peers earn significant money as an influencer on YouTube or on their blogs. It's evident each day on the form of their Insta feeds.

The main difference between previous generation and Gen Z is that the Gen Z has the means to make these goals reality. In middle school, a lot of them already have an extensive social media profile. People who start attracting an enormous audience instantly begin thinking about ways to use the power of social media and create a brand identity that is easily recognized.

The purpose of this talk is that Gen Zers are eager to expand, particularly financially. They know that they do not know everything, however, they're open to absorb as much information that they are able to. They'll be studying strategies you employ to promote your product or service... Be extremely well-informed on this point. You should also have the occasionally "how-to" blog or video that is targeted towards Gen Zers. Gen Zers love eating and eat that food.

4: You need to be more that just one

The millennial generation is extremely difficult to remain active. But they're not anything compared Generation Zers. In the average, millennials will have three screens (and occasionally switch among them). Gen Zers are able to bounce between five screens: smartphones, laptop television, desktop and tablet.

It is essential to understand. If your marketing strategy isto, for instance, display pre-roll ads through YouTube but the problem is that you won't get the attention of viewers. When the ads appear on their screens, their attention are already diverted to another device.

5. Tell the complete story in less than 8 seconds

This is the place we are right in the moment: an 8 second attention span. This is the standard among Gen Z users. If you're a Gen Zer, you need to be aware of this. If you wish your fellow Gen Zers who are interested in clicking your latest post, view your videos or follow your Insta images, you have to make them understand the purpose of your content what it is about, why they ought to care, and how it could make them smile or assist them.

And you must complete this in eight minutes or less.

This is an art that you're required to learn, and it could require a lot of time. Once you've mastered it, this method will pay well.

The next time we'll discuss ways to improve your capabilities being a Gen Zer and gain a competitive edge in your career.

Then, you can become Gen Zer

What are the requirements to be successful as Gen Zer? What are the steps to take to stand out from the the pack and reap greater profits than the rest of us? The most straightforward answer is: skills and knowledge. The skills you have will give you the edge you need. They help you become better at presenting yourself professionally, and can help you reach out to your target audience. The knowledge you acquire will allow you direct your talents towards the proper direction. This chapter will focus on the knowledge and skills that you require to succeed.

Essential Skills Required To Be Successful as a Gen Zer in A Market that is becoming increasingly crowded

Here are some skills you ought to consider learning:

1. SEO

For the majority of websites and marketing platforms on the internet SEO is by far the most popular sources of visitors. If you're not doing keyword research or coming up with optimised content, or constantly revising your website (this is the case for Facebook posts YouTube video content, Instagram post, and so on.) to ensure that SEO increases, be aware that there's another Gen Zer on the market who is your direct competition and doing these things.

2. Content Creation

Content creation is a skill that is actually learned. However, being a Generation Zer you probably already know this. The ability to come up with quality, value-added, and search-engine-optimized content is vital if you are to succeed in the online sphere as a Gen Zer. Content increases traffic, builds trust, and draws new clients and guides you on to.

3. Paid Adverts

While content is a great source of natural traffic, paying advertising is an extremely effective traffic source. Indeed, a large portion of Gen Zers who have made it to the top as professional in their field of expertise have tried paid advertising.

Many advertising platforms provide complicated targeting and filtering options that help you target customers a lot simpler and quicker. They also allow evaluation of whether your pages are effective, as well as the offerings of your products or services.

4. Accounting

Financial savvy is among the most essential skills you'll ever need. Being a Generation Zer you already have this knowledge. In fact, you probably teach this to your children. In your old age however, you might be unable to master the technical aspects of accounting required to totally transform the game to your advantage. Once you're familiar with the accounting concepts it will make you more at coordinating the financial aspects of your business. Things like tax-paying won't cause you to worry.

It is possible to take this up a notch by studying from those who are currently working in the field you'd like to become a specialist in. Nowadays, a majority of people prefer to learn about particular aspects of their lives from those who have actual experience or knowledge on the matter. In other words instead of taking an official class in which you'll learn ways to make money through wealth creation, you could sign up for an online class with someone who actively doing what the instructor teaches. This will give you more hands-on experience on the subject as compared to studying from a professor who hasn't tried what he/she's giving in the formal classroom.

Some of the locations where you can get a head start are:

Udemy.com

Teachable.com

Lynda.com (Now LinkedIn Learning)

Coursera.org

You can even flip the tables by putting together a course on something you've learned when you were younger and you'll be astonished by the number of people who could be searching for your expertise! Of course that for every product purchased there's a free version (even it's not as comprehensive). If funds for a paid course isn't readily available then you can look up online courses that are free. Let's talk about some classes you can take as a Gen Zer.

Work Assistance Gen Z Really Needs From Their Parents For Success

This chapter is different in that it's different from other chapters; it's mainly targeted at

Gen Zer parents, who are eager to be part of the process (of their children attaining and maintaining financial independence). This chapter is sure to be equally beneficial for Generation Zers... through studying it, they will understand how they can assist them in their success... in turn assist their parents in helping them" more effectively. It's a classic example of the well-known "help me assist to help" phrase. Therefore, with no further delay...

Gen Z is fixated on making sure that their financial future is secure and being accountable; this is obvious. This is why Gen Zers can already be farther than they are on the road to success than their parents were when they were their years of.

But it's important to recognize that although they're mature and responsible, Gen Zers are, they are still mostly kids. The most senior Gen Z crop is 21... Sure they've recently been able to drink alcohol However, they're vulnerable in various aspects of life and finance generally. They need guidance in order to reach their ambitions. It is also likely that parents will stand out of the way trying to offer the advice and guidance of a mature person. This chapter outlines how parents can lead the Gen Z kids toward success without hindering their growth and a ferocious spirit.

What's the next big scoop?

Absolutely, the Gen Zers will soon be entering the workforce when they turn 18 and achieve this with new goals and a new outlook. A majority of companies who are on the cutting edge will inform you that they anticipate Generation Zers to become like a breath of fresh air: effective focused, uncluttered, and advanced beyond their years.

Generations before them had traditional jobs. Considering how Gen Z has shaped up has also meant that they can hold traditional jobs. Financial security is the most important thing over everything else, not just the (and particularly) feelings. There are also endless opportunities and financial paths that exist besides the conventional ones. As technologically modern as Gen Zer are, they have the ability to explore the endless opportunities that are available that are available and earn money doing the things they enjoy doing at any time and from any location. According to the study of Upwork, at the very least, 47 % of Generation Zers are working and earning money through freelance work.

On the whole and you've got an concept of this by this point - Gen Zers are distinctly different from their millennial counterparts. Although millennials are often referred to as "the generation that flits between jobs," Gen Zers are more likely to remain with their employers for at least some time. The research conducted by The Chicago Tribune shows that more than 60 percent of them are likely to remain with a company for at least ten years.

The motives for Gen Zers are different than older generations too. Although many Gen Zers will openly admit they're focused on financial security more than all else, they'll mention advancement as a major reason. In this light it's easy to see why they're much more inclined to remain.

The development of career passions and fostering the entrepreneurial spirit of Gen Z Parent

1: Let them extend their wings

All children deserve varied experiences. Gen Zers are no different. They seek knowledge and will do whatever they can to acquire it and keep it. They can quickly absorb the happenings, not just in their own area, but also in distant places from where they are currently.

Parents should set the right foundation for their children by opening the doors to study subjects like architecture, performing arts as well as nature, culinary arts and various other traditions.

Let them experiment with "adult things," be it at the home or at work. For instance parents could let their children assist with furniture or home decorating choices. With tools such as Pinterest and Instagram Gen Zers have enough information to explore. Through this the parent is showing the Gen Z son/daughter that they have a serious approach to their interests and that they are confident.

2. Allow them to be able to

The environment in which children learn and play has seen a dramatic change throughout the past several years. It's been a long time since the brick-and-mortar borders that used to be the norm for learning and expression are not as important anymore. Instead of heading to the library for information or searching the classifieds section, Generation Zers have turned to phones. The majority of Gen Zers have smartphones. This fact has led to the Google algorithm that favors mobile websites.

Their lives are filled with virtual interactions like social media, for instance and other technologies that their parents weren't familiar with when they were children. Therefore, while reading news articles on Twitter or scouring Facebook boards for job opportunities might seem odd (or sensible) in the eyes of parents it's important to let your child discover information in places that they like and have a good understanding of. It is wrong to let parents dismiss social media as an unnecessary waste of time. Instead, they should inquire with their children where they get their information as well as what they read and what they decide to do with this information and give the kids plenty of opportunity to explore.

3. Allow them to fail, but do not

Risk-taking is essential... very essential. Parents must encourage Gen Zers into new areas that allow them to make errors. It's a problem that is causing a lot of people who are parents to Gen Z kids, perhaps inspired by the turbulence of the recent recession, are prone to overly shield their children even as their children reduce their efforts to be as safe as they can be. The result is a slowing growth. The millennial generation is difficult to critique in their enthusiasm for finances, education, and the general public however they did throw themselves into problems when they were children and could find solutions, while failing repeatedly. They were taught the art of grafting and making things from scratch. If another recession was to occur, it is logical to assume Gen Zers will be more impacted than millennials since they're less familiar with the art of innovation and grafting.

4: Be aware the fact that "when I was little kid" ..." does not work anymore

The parents have different opinions about the challenges that their Gen Z kids are facing. This is particularly true in the case of working. However, as knowledgeable and experienced as parents can be at a minimum when compared to their children it's an error to rely too much upon their (antiquated) experiences. Gen Zers don't like old stories. Some may inquire, with a smirk how the well-known advice stood up to the test in the years prior to and after the 2008 financial crisis (and the devastation they witnessed on their own).

Although parents are able to are trying with good intentions to influence their children's behavior as psychotherapist Sheryl Gonzalez Ziegler says, it's extremely easy for communication issues to arise.

This is a suggestion that can assist in transforming parents' parenting styles: teens are always looking for evidence that shows parents don't understand their needs. The use of instances from the past as a serious case study will helps to prove that you're operating in a different way.

It is best to rethink your position slightly; look into the Gen Zer's methods and strategies and then only criticize. You'll then be able to argue rationally and to do this backed by evidence. This can earn you a lot of points in the eyes of Gen Z teens. Gen Z teen.

Chapter 5: How To Know Generation Z

If you glance at the face of a Gen Z person these days What do you notice? Do you have a relationship (or more accurately, barely engage) in a way with someone locked in their bedroom in a quiet place, not even visible to you, and happy to be alone and unaffected?

But, do you know someone who is always online, with friends and family members streaming videos or playlists on their phones? With apps hooked up and connected to their smartphones Are they the generation that is disorientated and spending their time?

Who belongs to Generation Z?

When you refer to GENERATION Z, you are referring to those born between the years 1995 between 1995 and 2010. They constitute the demographic group which follows Gen Y, otherwise known as the Millennial Generation.

From the time they were children, they've not lived in a world that was without the internet and gadgets. Many of them were brought up by parents who were part of the Gen X and Millennials. What did it go for them growing as they grew up?

Unlike the Baby Boomers and Generation X who hovered over their kids, many members of Gen Z grew up in a "Figure-It-Out-Yourself" approach.

They're less sassy than the generations preceding them, due to the fact that they've experienced differently. Their parents were non-traditional families. They've witnessed gender roles change between their parents, all to boost the family's income. They've lived with Gen Y brothers and sisters and relatives who did not start and then returned to their homes.

More sarcastic and less cynical as their Millennial counterparts They are more sarcastic and less cynical. The Z Generation has a personality that is promising. Young adults, many are starting their first entry-level positions. Some are working as interns and waiting to be able to graduate from college.

Some are still at school, trying to figure out their identities and working to make the grade.

To comprehend what the Generation Z person is, you must first comprehend the world they live within. It's similar to saying you need to view the world through the eyes of the person.

Therefore, it's crucial to discuss them and in their presence, not as a participant in the room, but as an actual person who is a part of this conversation.

What is some of the Gen Z Lifestyle Habits?

Now, our discussion shifts to two key issues to address:

1. What is it that defines Gen Z's world? Gen Z?

2. What are the characteristics that differentiate them?

Welcom into the realm of INSTANT generation! This is a world of instant gratification, where you can access everything that is available. Everything is instant. The tools are there and you can get instant answers to any question.

In the same way that they come in and go out of your corner of the globe - within your influence as an adult or family member There are certain aspects of them that do not get overlooked. They are LIFESTYLE habits we associate with them and they are as follows:

1. They are mobile-savvy.

In addition to being technologically proficient this generation of mobile users is being mobile. Contrary to previous generations of Millennials who were interested in laptops, computers, as well as video gaming, the current group relies on phones chargers, batteries, and packs.

With multiple apps running at the same time, they're capable of watching movies on Netflix and stream music through Google Play or Spotify. All you need is one device that is the smartphone.

2. The people who admire them are the HEROIC.

In keeping with the superhero mindset of the current generation there are certain characteristics that they admire. In addition to being brave they are also daring. They are a fan of the speed of their thinking as well as quick-thinking. They are averse to bullies and will not tolerate any disrespect.

However they are fun and casual. Take them as an example of the characteristics of superheroes that the new generation is hoping to adopt.

3. They are an entirely different type of social.

We live in a time where interaction and socializing has been redefined. Socializing nowadays doesn't require getting out of the house to make friends and actually engaging with your circle of buddies. It's more about being locked into an area (usually in one's bed or room) and connecting to an online community of anyone who's online and active.

4. They are active and present online.

Most of the time, it's much more of an online profile rather than an in-person presence. When you've got guests over the son will be taking a bite of apple or going to the refrigerator for food before disappearing to his bedroom. Your daughter is slouching in her pyjamas for the entire day and then changing between messy and sexy in response to an SMS or a phone call.

If this is your life's story it's not an isolated story in this story. Around the globe these days, millions of families include young adults and teens that belong to this generation. This isn't unusual but it is.

At this point, it is important to keep in mind that although there are certain habits that are closely linked with Gen Z, there are also distinct differences. Gen Z, these habits shouldn't be generalized. Each person has their own distinct characteristic, and have different preferences. One of these options could be the possibility of becoming an Stoic.

Chapter 6: Understanding Their Behaviors

What are we actually aware of about the NEXT Generation? For Gen Z you can take this as an endorsement to identify you with iGen and the iGeneration. One step above Digital Native, you're Mobile Savvy. You're the best example of human evolution to date.

It's not just your mind and appearance that has changed. Your preferences and tastes have changed, too. Because we're very interested in your personality and the things you're capable of, enjoy us while we discuss the most fascinating details about you.

What Generations This Generation Wants

Let's think about it this way We're not quite sure how to comprehend Generation Y yet, but we're trying to figure out Generation Z. If we're going to be honest, we shouldn't depend on our personal opinions or hearsay from people around us. The best source of information is the informationgraphics that researchers and marketers have collected to broaden and enhance our understanding about Gen Z.

In order to help us create an unforgettable image of what the current generation is about, let's take an overview of five of the best informationgraphics to share:

1. Media consumption habits

Three areas are what we'd like to discuss and these include the gadgets they use, their time they watch TV, and the various social media they are using.

First off Gen Z and Millennials Gen Z are not identical in the way they use media.

From the most- to least-used, we'll classify the amount of time that Gen Y as well as Gen Z spend on their devices. Gen Z are: Desktops - Smartphone TV. Gen Z: TV - Smartphone Laptop.

* Gen Z spends less time on Facebook than Generation Y do. The most effective way to compete for attention could be other media such as Instagram or YouTube.

2. Shopping preferences

60% of Gen Z buyers prefer cool items over exciting experiences. Generation Z have distinct standards for the brands they purchase which are different from what Gen Y crowd is looking for.

Don't forget that teenagers have money and their buying power is massive.

3. Skills for work and recruiting

When the Baby Boomers age out the Generations X Z, Y, and X that "inherit" their work. But each generation has its own unique attitude and skill set.

For example, Gen Y scores high in passion, but a low score on teamwork. Gen Z sees the need to improve the management of people within the organization, but would like to start their own company. Based on research, this is equivalent into 75% teenagers who want to convert their interests into full-time employment. [ii]

4. Response to marketing

Traditional marketing campaigns don't be effective especially for Gen Z. They prefer ads that are visual, short and fun, but not snarky. They are those videos that become popular on their social networks.

5. Entertainment and culture

Being co-creators of culture The Z Generation doesn't only want to enjoy entertainment, but is also interested in shaping and making it. A vast potential that is not fully realized 60 percent from the Next Generation want to help transform the world as opposed to Millennials' 39 percent. [iii]

In the meantime, as the Next Generation continues to evolve and change, businesses need to learn more about this new and forthcoming workforce. Businesses and markets must keep providing goods and services that cater to the needs of this group.

If you can capture this market of consumers workers, consumers and creators of culture (or CC's) and imagine the impact that they will have on society, economy and the entire culture.

How they connect and communicate

Due to preconceived assumptions, many people believe that they're a boring and uninterested group. Much like their predecessors the Millennials were previously considered to be lacking determination and ambition.

Yet, if we desire to comprehend Gen Z better, we need to be able to communicate and be able to get through. To begin however, we need examine the notion of communication and examine what it is that has changed the present era:

1. Written and verbal skills

Without being overgeneralized the situation, it is clear that written and verbal communication skills aren't as well developed as older generations. They're not as adept at creating the correct spelling and grammar when writing an article or the text of a piece. However, do not think that they aren't creative enough. They're experts and whizzes in presenting and creating videos.

2. Texts versus emails

Generation Z is one who prefers to communicate via text messages rather than email. Gen Zers are intelligent enough to recognize the necessity of the use of an account on email. In the case of Yahoo and Google these accounts are essential for signing to games and chats.

3. User IDs and email accounts

Alongside email accounts, they need is Apple ID's. In addition, they need additional User ID accounts, which give them access to many websites and apps. These websites and apps are not just for video and games but as well to selling and shopping online.

4. Online messaging

In addition to texting via text messages or via instant messenger, users have different alternatives. It's equally easy to connect with online messengers which is the most well-known of which is Facebook Messenger. Nowadays, it's common for many teens to be part of a variety of Facebook groups.

5. Facebook groups

These groups aren't just group of people who talk about nothing, as we usually think. There are groups that gather together and organize their social activities. They consist of peers and classmates who talk about political and social questions. There are groups with the same passion for sports, and then there are groups that are business-oriented. We're talking about companies that allow users to build profiles, create reputations, and exchange or trade items for fun or in exchange for cash.

6. Experience on Instagram

Well, it's ok. With increasing numbers of than one parent "invading" Facebook, Generation Z has somehow chosen to reduce their utilization of Facebook. Facebook no longer seems to be their preferred place for socializing and posting So don't assume you've got everything done. If you've been disenfranchised with the changes (and through the various apps, too) It would be a good idea to brush up on the latest information. Instagram has become the most popular platform for Generation Z.

7. Selfies and Snapchats

The most important thing about Instagram is its uniqueness and its privacy. The Instagram generation loves quick posts about some new experience that they had in the last few minutes. (It's it's the Instant Generation that you remember?) You could take a picture taken by yourself, or with a group of friends (and the photo bomber) or pets doing hilarious and funny routines. If you don't share Instagram images on Facebook the memories are short, infrequent and therefore private.

When you begin to panic It's not always about you being the adult. Your child isn't "evading" you , and you lose your place on Facebook. The upside is that being on and off of Instagram is beneficial to them. It can help prevent many of the common negative experiences that the previous generation experienced (and continue to endure) from Facebook which includes bullying and cyberbullying.

In a constantly-explicit and critical world that doesn't know the lines or values their boundaries, it is easy to be a victim of snobs. They are bullies that could easily ruin the reputation of a person and their self-esteem.

Consider your IG incident as being a crucial but flawed solution. It's for a generation that would like to not be subject to issues like social stigma. Particularly for those who lived in an environment that is rife with conflict at home or a sense of discrimination within communities, IG becomes a safer area, with less drama.

8. Sharing and following

Another characteristic of Gen Z is the fact that they know what's popular. They are inclined to FOLLOW and SHARE. If they've noticed something or someone that's interesting and fresh, they notice the sign. Then they're an observer.

One among the top types of media that Gen Z to share and follow is videos that focus on the joy of failure and fun. There's something to be said about the most epic failures that Gen Z really enjoy watching.

NOVELTY. PRIVACY. PLEASURE. FAILURE. What is the Stoic's view regarding these failures? What are they "good" as opposed to "bad" according to your perspective?

If we do we'll also have to deal in seeking pleasure with immediate gratification. There are times when instant gratification may not be enjoyable however, the things that are pleasurable don't have to be immediately available. Between the two you must strike the right balance. In the end, there's something that Stoics refer to as MODERATION and this is also beneficial.

In Part 2 there's plenty to say about forming in groups. While the concept of sharing, following and getting along are two aspects of what Gen Z is made of but they leave a gap that needs filling. This emptiness of life can leave a lot of us young people feeling agitated unhappy, discontented, angry and a bit sad.

At the beginning, think of this as an opportunity to live your life with something that is meaningful! If you decide towards becoming a Stoic one, you'll lead healthier, happier and yes, quieter ones. If you decide to stop being as a follower and you are ready to lead.

Allegiant, divergent or whatever or are, you'll be able to discern the right and right. Changes for the good can be made by a person who is able to learn the benefits of Stoicism.

This is how we'd close this chapter: In the myriad of traits we typically refer to as Gen Z

Generation Z, do we ever use the word "CHARACTER?

Character, as a characteristic is a characteristic that determines the individual. It is a sign of strength and motivation. For his part, Epictetus exemplified what it means to demonstrate strength in character. As an slave, he held the following thought: "I laugh at those who believe that they are damaging me. They don't even know what I'm about and they don't even know my thoughts and they are unable to be able to touch things that belong to me and the things I live by." He did go as a free man and then become one of the most important Stoic philosophers of his day.

In the above example you can see how vital it is to develop the character within yourself (in this instance the your character) before you are able to endure any external suffering and hardship. The good news is that character as a personal characteristic can be developed and refined through the years of practice and time which is precisely the kind of thing we're supposed to discover in the 2nd part of this ebook.

Chapter 7: The Traits That Are Associated

With Adulthood

The large portion of Gen Z is composed of young adults who are in their teens until their early 20s. It's not possible to talk to them as if they're kids because they're not children anymore but you aren't able to handle them as fully-grown adults as well, since they're still growing up. They're in the process what's now known as "ADULTING."

It is important not to smuggle the young adults in our lives and undervalue their potential. Since they'll be the adult children in the near future - and that translates to our future globe - it's important to know the way they think and feel.

As with emotions and the aging process naturally, you can experience extreme emotions. If emotions are intense and unruly, they can be prone to take over all the rational thoughts.

In this scenario it's the capacity to manage one's own self and manage your emotions that will be the most important thing. As

Seneca was so well-written in his Morals of a Happier Life Benefits, Anger and Clemency "All acts of violence are the result of vulnerability." If your weakness was anger, it could result in you being rude, cruel and violent toward other people. The most important thing, then as Stoics believe , is to control your anger and limit it as passion.

What do these young Adults Think

Contrary to what the majority of people think there aren't any teenagers who are wild and inexplicably unpredictable. They experience different emotions and thoughts which affects the way they choose to do (action) and the way they act (behavior).

But, even among youngsters, they are inclined to behave in various ways. Some tend to be more social and outgoing while others are more reserved and introverted. Some people are more flexible and relaxed, while some are focused and shrewd. Certain people can handle the burden with ease, whereas others require more effort and guidance. In ideal circumstances it would be easy to bring them up from toddlers to adults, provided we knew them as individuals.

In this ebook, we will try to discover how these young adults feel and think according to what their culture has taught them.

It's true. A majority of people in the next generation like to get their information from peers instead of from adults. In particular, when it comes down to advice and tips Most likely, they prefer to hear it from someone who been through the same experience and has walked in the similar shoes.

When it comes to shoes, it seems that the current generation is afflicted with a distinct obsession with shoes. They're the kind of individuals who think it is possible to tell something about someone by their shoes and how they dress. So, a man could wear a simple pair of jeans and a t-shirt however it's his shoes that tell tales about him.

8 traits that define Gen Z

What is it that makes Gen Z tick? What are the factors that make them the way they are? In addition to the normal behaviors they've acquired, like constant sharing, texting, as well as streaming videos, how else do we know about their personality?

To help you comprehend this generation more clearly Here are eight TRACTS that clearly define how the generation is thinking and feeling

1. INDEPENDENCE

Already Gen Z's already have the traits of the Stoic. They're strong-willed and self-sufficient. Their potential is not fully realized.

So far, they're quite happy with their use of technology, which has helped them become very independent. Fast to grasp instructions (note that they are not able to read) and don't have to depend upon their elders to use it or navigate the system.

Ironically parents are more likely to depend on their children to show them (as as patiently or quickly as is possible) the way things functions. There isn't much talk about software nowadays; the focus is on apps.

2. CONFIDENCE

It requires confidence to defend the things you believe in. Stoics are courageous and confident by their very nature.

In this generation, they're not just great navigators, but they're also more confident. There's no longer a time where we would second-guess ourselves about whether we understood the right instructions or not.

For the current generation, they push ahead, work out the little details later and face the challenges as they arise. Sometimes they will require affirmation However, the majority of the time they get right into it. If we are able to remember that they're focused on being young.

3. ENRREPRENEURSHIP

As they grow up and become self-sufficient, they are extremely ENTREPRENEURIAL. Entrepreneurs who begin from a young age are likely to prove efficient and conscious of costs. They may be very efficient in managing money.

4. Creativity

With the ability to think outside of boundaries, people possess the potential to be creative. It is evident in their literature, music and art. Because they are easily distracted, but it's sometimes difficult to keep their focus. They have a difficult time trying to stay focussed on the task in hand (unless it's an activity or gadget). They're too dependent on technology and gadgets as they've never lived life in any other way.

5. LOYALTY

As consumers and buyers They are extremely loyal. They don't choose any brand, apart from the one that is a match for their fashion sense and enthusiasm. It is because of their help and support that a brand can enjoy such a large fan base.

Imagine the changes that could occur in the next generation if they were to stand firm to their beliefs and what is good. It could be the beginning of a massive shift in our thinking towards one that is more Stoic one.

6. FASHION SENSE

They are incredibly trendy. Because they're up-to-date with the latest trends, these are the ones who will be willing to spend money or trade other things to obtain the most up-to-date and trendiest. This is top-of-the-line because this generation will not accept less.

However, without being too general there are a few of them who aren't too enthusiastic about trends and brands. These are the people who opt to keep it simple and remain savvy when it comes to spending money.

7. PASSION

This means that a lot of this generation have become brand-conscious. According to the concept of branding, people don't require many things to make them feel happy however, they might require plenty of a specific sort of item that they're enthusiastic about.

Referring to our previous illustration, Gen Z teenagers may like sporting the exact hoodie repeatedly and over and it doesn't be a big deal to them if their friends (and indeed their parents) think they're a particular kind of. But If they're interested in a specific kind of brand of clothes all the time, it's when the enthusiasm be displayed. They'll certainly be talking about caps and sneakers as well as boots and heels.

If they're passionate about something, they'll discover a way to maintain the passion as a hobby regardless of whether or not they ask. When a mini collection is established and grew, it could become a plethora of lipsticks and makeup, as well as a plethora of other items.

The issue with this kind of obsession is that they are consumerism. It is a waste of time energy and energy. You leave with a label and brand of products, but you they don't leave a lasting impression on the good work you've done to the world. Therefore, even though they may be satisfying, they're useless. They are not meaningful. Next Generation can succeed in life, but only by doing something worthwhile.

For Gen Z the most important factor is whether they are happy with this or dislike it. If they aren't happy with it, they will not pursue it. They'll not even give it a chance to be a part of their day. If they really like it, it's going to be evident. It's not even necessary to convince them to achieve the end goal. Furthermore the information will be shared with followers and groups of social networks.

As sophisticated and smart as young adults can be but they're rough on the outside. As a result of character development it is essential that they are refined by the passage of experience and life.

What they think about life generally

After exploring how youngsters think, it's now time to discover what they are feeling. As we're from a different generation in general, we may perceive as being a bizarre creatures that do strange things.

All of these quirks are not meant to cause us to be isolated from one another however. Instead we'll be able connect by understanding their feelings about life in the following manner:

1. The classic fairytale that is a vivid stories instead of the realities of reality, some children are raised to believe that they'll be successful or, more precisely it's instant.

2. If the majority of activities are virtual it is easy to fall out of the reality. Virtual reality isn't quite like the simple and unambiguous reality. Generation Z may have unrealistic

expectations of life that are challenging even to live up to.

3. Many people are raised in isolated lives in tight environments that cause them to become individualistic. Contrary to the chattering on social media or social media, they might be quiet and quiet at home. Instead of being open to people around them, they might retreat to a quiet, secluded behavior and quiet.

4. For children who haven't been taught to be compassionate and kind, some develop into self-centered and selfish. So, we're completely clueless and are then shocked to discover that we've bred an image-centric generation that is susceptible to be aggressive and self-centered. Narcissism is a form of self-love that is extreme. It's an insincere and egotistic love of oneself beyond all reason.

5. Studies show that this generation in which many suffer from signs of attention deficit disorder. A more acquired form of inattention and lack of focus, this disorder is all too prevalent. It has several possible causes, but one is excessive activity. In the midst of a flurry of activities that aren't suitable for their

age, children exhibit signs of uncontrolled behavior.

6. In the present we are dealing with an entire generation of kids who are grown-up, but often unfocused by their impatience, impulsive, and indecisive. However, there are people who are becoming increasingly nervous, uneasy, and irritable and more likely to be at times depressed or agitated.

How Does This Generation Deal with Stress

To gain an understanding of what they are feeling inside We must find out what's stressing them out. Do they feel stressed because of the routine at school and home? Are you feeling pressure from peers? Are the demands of society? Perhaps it is an unsolved issue or problems in them that cause negative conduct?

In reaction to stress, teens might begin to binge and overeat. They might stop exercising or work on self-care. They may stop going out with their friends , or cut them out completely. They may even be drawn into drinking, smoking or using drugs and other vices.

There are always WARNING SIGNS (like those above) which tell us when it's become too to much for a teenager. These RED FLAGS aren't as easily discernible however, particularly when we are discontent and distracted by our lives.

In the case of Gen Z How do you cope with the stress of your life? Do you rise to the challenge or do you give up whenever you face difficulties? Do you envision yourself going through a difficult time without complain?

If we hear a lot of grumbles Do not be concerned. There is no need to worry. We are not either critical or judgmental. We have been Gen Z; we are Stoic. Take that all together and we'll be virtually invincible!

But underneath that armor an Stoic is built, there was a person who was struggling to become free. What exactly is freedom from? Yes, there is something called FREEDOM FROM passion. One reason is that when stress affects you inside and you are afflicted, you suffer. From mildly anxious to extremely depressed, you are suffering from an obsession that Stoics refer to as distress.

In the majority of cases, however passions tend to be about the stress (or tensions and discords) that occur whenever we experience an overwhelming urge or need. Some of these desires are healthy, however, as we'll discover as we move on to Stoicism in Part 2.

In the end, regardless of what, STRESS is a normal element of our lives. According to the Stoics the distinction lies in how you manage stress and how you don't let it impact you.

The process of becoming an adult doesn't end here. In Part 2 we'll discover that being an adult is more than just getting rid of stress. It is more than that. It is about overcoming difficulties and maintaining determination when difficulties arise. There are many who struggle however not everyone is capable of overcoming and enduring. We'll take from Stoicism however we will put it off until Part 2 to clarify.

Chapter 8: Teaching The Next Generation

How do you know the current generation of students on the campuses of colleges in the present? To guide and teach them to be successful Are you aware of the method to employ as well as how you can prepare them to their job?

If it's been years since you (or did not) complete your education and you don't have any desire to go back to university in any way, then you may have lost contact with this crowd. The rhythm of this crowd differs than yours, and they're now hearing the beat of a different drummer.

Drum roll please! Prepare for the new generation of graduates and our future workforce. Gen Z is the current generation of students on colleges in the present. It is a group who values education, however their priorities and needs have changed. This shift in thinking is the thing that teachers, parents and counselors should be aware of.

Generation Z Heads to College

Like everyone who has gone between high school and college, the phase of deciding can be difficult! As you are attempting to achieve the term "Higher Education All your senses are on the rise. A student may already be stricken by the expense of education as well as the cost on student loan. They may be worried about receiving the right scholarship or even not.

If you're reading this through the perspective of a parent you may be drowning in debt and mortgage. It's no joke how youngsters and their families are facing, especially when it comes to finances.

To help you get into college Did your parents or yourself as a parent participated in an excursion to campus recently? When you are on an educational tour one of the first things you will notice is that there is not an admin or instructor that runs the tours. Instead, it's an individual PEER - also known as Gen Z - who's part of the students.

The reason for this is that the fellow Gen Z student is considered to be a more trustworthy sources of knowledge. Because the information they share is something that students have experienced this experience is considered to be valid. The peer is perceived as someone who they can really be able to identify and connect with.

What mentoring styles work best?

As a mentor for the next generation What are the best ways to lead your in the right direction? What method do you choose to use?

Simply put, the old-fashioned approach will not work any longer. There's a lot that can say about the education and discipline that they might had received, there's more about motivation and inspiration that you can offer them.

Have you thought about how you can aid an Gen Z relative or friend achieve success in life? It's similar to the method by the counsellors and teachers could assist.

1. The first step is to create a stronger motivation to encourage their students to engage and taking part in the discussion. It is essential to involve them. In the event that they don't, they'll block you out.

2. It's not enough to simply command and for them to comply. You must give them more than this. It is important to earn their trust and respect.

3. As an educator, it's crucial to find the right balance between your thoughts and their input. As much as you would like to be heard to, they too want to be listened. Although they may be quiet and indifferent, however they appear to be, you must be attentive to their desire to be heard and seen.

4. It is not a good idea to mentor by imposing yourself or your ideas from the position of authority, but rather by gaining CREDIBILITY. Similar to the older model is more trustworthy by speaking from an expert's knowledge rather than from personal experience.

5. In your teaching, demonstrate MASTERY in your subject. When you're asked for advice, make it short and straightforward. The world has changed so that lengthy, long-winding tales are not going to help anyone in today's Instant Generation.

6. Do not forget that this is an inquisitive and intelligent group. So, expect their questions to

be more detailed and technical. You may want to focus on the answer not just by making declarations, but also through the use of illustrations and graphs.

7. When counselling is required the school counselors who play a crucial role. Since they are school personnel who engage with students on a every day or on a per-need basis They are expected to keep information confidential.

8. Counsellors should also not be just pleasant and chatty. They must be able to listen and provide the best SUPPORT. When one understands what motivates and inspires these youngsters they can be properly motivated them and help them meet their individual requirements.

9. An assessment of skills can be a great help, too. Based on the test results you can help them to careers that develop their entrepreneurial abilities. Additionally, there are those who use their financial expertise.

10. For a more practical (and cost-effective) To be more practical (and economical), provide students with resources that they can access online. The students require

documents can be saved to flash drives as well as memory cards.

11. As per #10, do not use the old-fashioned way of giving them handouts made of paper. Why? It is because all of the documents and photocopies pile up in the form of CLUTTER in their rooms. Instead, assist parents and children (do I feel the sound of relief?) to lessen the clutter around the home , and also to develop the practice of minimalism.

MINIMALISM goes beyond living a minimalist, simple life. It is also about making your life easier by reducing the amount of clutter. If you'd like to know more about the simple life of the Stoic lifestyle, then head to Part 2. In the meantime, join us as we assist in reorienting all of us on how we can employ the young.

How to Reorient their thinking

In terms of work The workplace can be an emotional minefield. It can be extremely stressful. All over the world, you will find anger and passions that are volatile. So, how do you manage, conquer and persevere?

To enable Gen Z workers to be able for Gen Z worker to survive in this environment They must be built of stronger materials. Also, they must learn better social skills since these are the types of situations they'll be facing:

1. It's not just one you work in. In the present, your workplace could be a COMPLEX environment that you must bridge (and traverse) gaps in generation.

2. No matter if whether you're Gen Z or not, you'll be part of a close group with other generations. At the time of this writing it is likely that there are five generations in total that is: X and Y Z, the 80's Generation, the Baby Boomers, as well as the old Traditionalist Generation.

3. So, the avoidance behaviour that many of us habitually accustomed to just won't work anymore. It is necessary to improve your interaction. You must work with individuals from diverse backgrounds in terms of education and socio-economics.

4. Although it's okay to use Instagram and Facebook at breaks and lunch, it's not acceptable to make use of your smartphone at work. While working the distractions of

your mobile are not just a source of irritation for your coworkers and managers however, they can also be danger to your safety. Beware!

5. If you're strong-minded and self-sufficient, don't worry about when you're under supervision. SUPERVISION is a fundamental part of the job, and your job in the company.

6. While businesses do their best to change to the latest technology, not every IDEA can be implemented immediately. If there are established operating procedures in place, they are simply required to be followed.

7. Although any SUGGESTION is always welcomed however, there's a specific appropriate time and location for it. It's not prudent to make a casual comment or arguing with your boss, so be sure to take your time!

8. It is also not advisable to categorize people according to the generation they are a part of. Thus, you should give them the chance. The best way to approach it is to concentrate at the best qualities of every person as well as to encourage cohesion and unity at work.

TACT. CAUTION. FOCUS. HARMONY. These are terms that are heavily linked to Stoicism. If you'd like to know more, skip to Part 2. If you're interested in how to attract the most talented talents to work for your company make sure you go through our section on recruiting.

Chapter 9: Providing Guidance To Students In Career Options

Are Gen Z's members Gen Z set on their professional path? If yes, which colleges are they considering?

A point to take note of is that more of Generation Z are opting for community colleges. There is no longer a time when everyone wanted to go to that Ivy League and competed for it. Today's youth have become more pragmatic about money, and even scrubbing about their living space and their board.

Not just a popular choice it's a practical option. It's designed by Generation Z individuals who are more conscious of their spending. Be aware of the ways that student loans and debt that is not consolidated will impact their lives later on They are much more cautious when making investments. It is no doubt that they are looking to maximize their worth from education.

So, you can anticipate Gen Z to shop around for colleges before they decide to apply. In contrast to the past, it's no longer possible to be a random college that they enroll in. Nowadays it's the norm that it must be a school that they choose.

How do you Recruit the Best Gen Z Talents

Employers, are you prepared to hire from the new talent pool? Do you think there are any candidates?

The positive side is that Gen Z-ers seem to be more engaged in the workplace as Millennials were. But, keep in mind that "they're interested in working isn't the same as 'you bringing them to go to work'. Therefore, if you're looking to get the best among the bunch of this generation to be working for you, you must improve your game plan.

1. It's helpful to are able to access a mobile application to make hiring easier. Do not engage them in a circular method with boring letters and repeated emails. Instead, entice them with short but engaging texts and apps that appeal to the audience.

2. If you're looking to recruit the best among Gen Z, then avoid the temptation to bombard them with automated email. Most companies today are able to sell their services by using email marketing. They respond with an auto responder to all job applications.

The campaign of sending the same message to every and every request is not effective. It is an absolute turnoff for those who are Gen Z applicant. It's uninteresting and boring.

3. In addition, numerous repeated emails can be frustrate. They can only fill up the inbox. Whatever you add in quantity, you might not be as thorough. So, ensure you are able to provide quality content.

4. In recruiting people from those in the Gen Z workforce, SPEED is crucial! If they do actually respond to you, offer them immediate feedback. Remember you are in an Instant Generation, therefore immediate feedback is the best way to go.

5. In the case of questions related to work What Gen Z candidates require is an PERSON on the other side of the spectrum. That means someone who is able to provide

answers and answer their questions immediately.

6. If you are responding to an applicant an applicant, your response doesn't have to be "Yes" either "No." The answer "Maybe" might be well appreciated, provided you inform them of the areas you'd like to improve. Don't be vague when it comes to this either. Be specific and clear about what you'd like to achieve in order to make sure that you're all on the same with the same.

7. Last but not least, utilize your PERSUASION skills. What if you've successfully attracted the most influential and popular in Gen Z? Since these are the people with a massive following, you won't require any advertising to grow. Through the power of word-of-mouth and the power of sharing (because this is exactly the way Gen Z does so well) Your marketing campaign can go viral!

How to Keep them Interested at Work

Are you concerned about how your new employees are going to behave in the office? Are they going to answer the request to go to work? Once you've hired them how can you keep them?

The most important thing is qualities like patience and resourcefulness. Find ways to grab their attention and keep it. In the beginning, you might not be able to hold it for very many minutes, so ensure that you make the most of every moment.

As interest changes and fluctuates so you need to maintain it. Here's how you can keep them motivated at work, regardless of how well-known they may be for having a sluggish attention span.

1. Create a fun environment! Make sure to bring the element of entertainment to your work. It's important to make the process enjoyable. For example, by employing a method known as Gamification Let the process of earning credits and points become a kind of game. They'll enjoy it!

2. Train them how to MIX or MINGLE. As a generation exposed to social media expect to see them less team-oriented and social initially. Make sure to create a sociable atmosphere where individuals work on their own and also working in groups.

3. Utilize to the practice of PEOPLE Engagement. Participate in group activities that encourage group spirit and occasionally playing. Create a workplace that is not overly frequent and time-consuming for them but it could be exhausting to the true Gen Z.

4. Returning to TIME Try to make the schedule more flexible. If work can be accomplished in flexi-hours, and with breaks that are scheduled, test it. If it's successful it will result in an entire group of content, happy employees who believe it's a relief to know that demands from their job aren't overly demanding and lengthy.

5. Another thing Did you think about making sure your employees are happy and healthy? Since food is one of their biggest pleasures, think about ways to care for your employees in this area.

In the term "arena," we are referring to an office cafeteria with snacks and meals, a fully-stocked shelves with their favourite snacks, and unlimited cups of coffee and fluids to stay going and well-hydrated.

These are only a few of the ways you can attract the top of your new talent and keep them interested. It's not necessary to scratch your head for too long about how you can please your employees and keep them feel happy. Many of the solutions you require are in your reach and are readily available. Learn right from the Gen Z.

Chapter 10: Gen Z And Social Problems

In the previous chapter we spoke about engagement with people in the workplace. There are many ways you can get individuals to make them more attracted to their work and enjoy it.

This is also true for social problems. It is possible to engage Generation Z into becoming more socially aware. The trick is to connect with them on a personal level and bring out their love for social consciousness.

Social awareness is a talent that Stoics are skilled at. Because service is one of the tenets that Stoicism is founded on It is a skill that Gen Z should learn to develop.

Be Social, but Keep Real

Before you can show your social consciousness it is necessary to overcome social media. Social media is what keeps people awake all night long and even into the early dawn hours.

Growing up in a society where, generally it is the standard, people have a strong belief that it's an essential feature they cannot live without.

As connected as they are in a technological and digital level, it can remind them that not all connections are actually real. The majority of them are virtual connections to people who aren't aware of them, aside from tiny tidbits of information they communicate.

Therefore, encourage the children to create real, long-lasting bonds. Inspire them to form bonds with their parents and other family members. Engage them with activities that give one another genuine smiles and not ones that are only for show.

We're all social Another thing for Gen Z to learn from the Stoics is to be mindful of their privacy. The approval is one aspect but respect is a different thing.

Let them know that there's more to be done in life that just hanging on the internet for hours. Real life awaits. Every once in awhile it's fine to get rid of their devices for a while and simply enjoy the wonderful outdoors .....

Be aware that no Generation is as connected and active as Generation Z. They're a ready audience that is waiting to be reached! Don't let this potential get lost by limiting them to the image of an uninterested, lazy bunch. Like every person who keeps surprising you, you're sure to be surprised!

The Issues They Find Engaging

Don't undervalue the potential that is Your Gen Z audience. According to statistics, there are over 350 million people who are of Gen Z age. Marketers estimate that they comprise around 25.9 percent of the population. With a population of millions, this audience is translated into hundreds of likes, comments and shares that grow exponentially.

The most important thing is: What are the issues that the people of this generation care about? In general, what issues are they all concerned about and how does help be used to benefit the world?

1. Racial inequality issues

On a global scale the next generation has more strongly the need for equality of opportunities and racial equity. Particularly for those who've been taught to be more open in their perception and not prejudicing regarding people and have more understanding of the concept of diversity. As a result of the process of change they are more open to different perspectives on race, color as well as language and culture.

2. Pets and pets are the most important thing to consider.

The present generation is one of goodwillers. One of the most effective methods to bring their enthusiasm into the world is to talk about pets. Pet care is what brings this generation to life. They're the best option to contribute to pet funds as well as other movements that are related to animals. Therefore, let them feel as if they're part of something meaningful and sensible, like Pet Rescue or Habitat for Humanity.

3. Conservation of nature

Another issue that Gen Zers will be a part of is environmental issues and conservation. It's going to be their world, after all, and it's now their responsibility to protect their natural resources.

Particularly in regions where youngsters are well-traveled, they've already discovered a wider world. They're also capable of recognizing beauty and the beauty of nature.

However, with a few exceptions we're talking about generation with an opportunity to become more sensible as well as less emotionally driven. In addition to being driven to succeed They are equally passionate about the world in their own ways.

To contact them, you need to know what websites and apps they frequently use and which websites they frequently. If you'd like them to help a cause, make sure to visit the forums they're on like YouTube or WhatsApp.

It's possible that we've dissuaded them from spending time on Facebook isn't it? It's because FB is now an adult playground. It's less likely that they'll be using Twitter or Viber as well, due to the fact that they belong to an older (read older) generation.

Instead, search for Snapchats or Instagram posts as they are the places where they are expressing themselves. It's where they go not just to be noticed however, but to also be heard. If they are satisfied with what they hear and see from you, then please you for the blessings of your stars! In a short time they'll be mobilizing their resources and promoting your cause. In only a few clicks you've already reached out to an audience that is capable of bringing change and changing the world!

Here are the questions you have to answer:

1. If you're Gen Z yourself, what concerns are you most are passionate about?

2. What causes would you like to support to change the world?

3. How can you do your part in liberating the world from the drama and conflict which cause so much pain?

If you've completed these questions and are now ready to take a leap, let's proceed. Go to the next page to discover how you can bring about positive change around the globe starting with a simple movement known as STOICISM.

Chapter 11: Learn To Be Aware Of The Stoic

In You

When we close the book and start a new chapter, our focus will be focused on YOU. You are an individual belonging to Generation Z. Next Generation. It could also be you as a family member or friend connected to someone who's Gen Z.

In our introduction we'll combine our previous questions: How do you, regardless of whether you're Gen Z or not Gen Z, achieve making a better living for yourself and your loved ones? It starts by knowing the meaning of what Stoicism is and implementing its principles.

Recognize Your Potential to Be Stoic

If you're keeping track of the latest trends, you'll be aware of the fact that there's a lot of discussion taking place about Stoicism. Do you know that you can become an Stoic as you begin your journey as a person who is bold and independent?

There is clearly the resurgence of Stoicism in the modern world of thought. An era of mobilizing people to make a change, and it's reaching out across generations, especially to Generation Z.

To look at the demographics, one group of America U.S. says that:[v]

You're an individual that is mobile-savvy. You are more active online. Therefore, you are able to inspire people to changes.

* You have less time in front of the television when in comparison to previous generations. Most of your time is spent on smartphones and gadgets which are more enjoyable.

As independent as you are you're more inclined to the entrepreneurial path. You'll be the leaders of the future.

• As a business-oriented person you are more cautious about risk. You're less certain about the economic situation.

You're connected to your friends. Through your social media and groups there is a huge network of people to follow and share.

It is more probable for you to form new friendships. You have acquaintances and friends from different ethnic, cultural religious, and racial groups.

This is because your mind is more open notion of the diversity of race. You've been taught to be more socially conscious.

* You have an ancestral family that is not as traditional and non-traditional. There are some who are single parents or identical-sex families.

* You are part of an age group that is willing to explore new concepts. You are able to pose questions and seek answers, you're not only religious , but also a philosophical.

With all the above it is possible to become an affluent Stoic.

Who else is into Stoicism?

Before you there were philosophers from the past along with famous and renowned leaders that learned and taught Stoicism. As shakers and movers of the past they used it as an ethical code for living by.

If you're bored of the history of this book, you can skip this section and continue through the chapter. If you're looking for an understanding of The Ancient Stoics and the people who followed them, then continue reading.

Zeno from Citium was the father of the Stoic school of philosophy. He was an affluent merchant who, during a journey between Phoenicia to Piraeus and back, survived the wreck of a ship, but was lost.

Seneca was a Roman politician, Seneca served as adviser to the Emperor Nero. He was the source of Senecan Thought - a Stoic writing that helped to shape generations upon generations of like-minded philosophers.

A major personage in Stoic time, Epictetus rose from being born a slave , to become among the top and most powerful philosophers of his day. He started his own school that taught the fundamentals, and wrote books on them.

The acclaimed Roman Emperor and famous general Marcus Aurelius, was a fan of the ideas of Epictetus. He kept a diary of his Stoic observations and these reflections were collected into a book called "Meditations."

In addition to the two of you, how many others is interested in Stoicism? To provide you with a hint about who to follow, here are some well-known people who are open about reading about Stoicism:

Frederick the Great the King of Prussia was more than just read about the topic. He stored the documents in his saddlebags to motivate him during the midst of sudden disaster.

In the group of founding fathers among the founding fathers, it is George Washington and Thomas Jefferson who embraced Stoicism close. It's not an accident that many of your schools are named in honor of the two.

When it comes to Stoicism the most famous English philosopher of the 19th century is believed to include John Stuart Mill. Mill was a writer on the quest for happiness and pleasure through the lens of freedom and logic.

* Albert Ellis was a 20th-century psychologist who initiated an era of change by introducing

the idea of Cognitive Behavioral Therapy (CBT). Informed by Stoic theory, this method has been applied to a variety of conditions which require not only treatment for depression and anxiety and addiction, but also rehabilitation from addiction.

* A lover of Epictetus along with Marcus Aurelius, John Sellars was an academic as well as philosopher. He wrote two acclaimed books on the impact of Stoic thinking on our lives. This put Stoicism within the perspective of our choices in our contemporary world.

* Which of your favorite writers are today's Stoics? Include on your list some famous names like Ralph Waldo Emerson and John Steinbeck. Emerson was particularly famous for his wide-ranging perspective on Stoicism and this was apparent in his writings, poems, essays and other writings.

When he returned after during the Vietnam War, James Stockdale described in a book how he managed endure all the trials required to become a prisoner of war. In captivity, Stockdale remained true to the lessons of life shared by Epictetus (as an slave) and survived.

*In the East, Stoic thinking has been influencing the present Prime Minister in China, Wen Jiabao. He claims that he has been through "Meditations" written by Marcus Aurelius over a hundred times.

There are many modern-day individuals who claim to adhere to the principles of Stoicism However, none of them is so well-informed and influential as the people we've listed above. With their stellar reputations alone it is impossible to have stated the truth more clearly.

Stoicism is, however, not exclusively reserved for the older philosophers and great writers. Even today, and at certain points of your lives, it's an idea that might be suitable for you. If you're eager to learn what Stoicism is and the way it came into being in the first place, then read the next page.

Chapter 12: Uncover The Meaning Of

Stoicism

Like a rite It requires an age-specific level and degree of maturity to reach Stoicism as a solution. While it was around for a long time, on the horizon through each generation, it's made its grand return today.

It is most likely this generation of people who are the most in need of Stoicism and that's why people are more open. People are responsive because they perceive an urgent need to the change. Reason suggests that Stoicism is a solid and rational solution to the challenges our world is confronting in the present. Because Stoicism is a seamless blend of the philosophies of Buddhism, Islam, and Christianity as you'll observe that it's an option that is attainable no matter what religion or age you're in.

Additionally, people become conscious of Stoicism's ideals Stoicism after they've been confronted with difficulties. When tragedy strikes, Stoicism is like a rock. It is a Stoic philosophy to keep you grounded and strong from the inside. Life-changing experiences form and shape you until you can become a Stoic. Once your character is established and you are able to stand the test of time, you will never be shaken.

What is Stoicism? How can it be defined?

Many people believe that Stoicism is a brand emerging movement. It's a type of new age thought that people are becoming into. This definition could be misleading.

As an individual, you could be a part of this thinking and even be termed modern-day STOIC. Stoics are those who aren't driven or controlled through their feelings. They are not averse to pleasure and pain or grief and joy they act in a rational, unaffected manner. If we take this definition, it isn't in accordance with what Stoicism completely is about.

In the beginning, STOICISM was initially used as a concept of philosophy. It is a method of thinking. It implies that the most fundamental questions concerning the nature of the universe and life have been considered and asked, and the responses have been researched and debated. The whole thing has been thought-through and thoughtfully formulated.

As a philosophy that dates back to the beginning of time that was a part of the ancient world, this school of thought is founded on the moral principles and virtues that we'll explore in a moment. One of the ancient philosophies is Eudaemonism where you achieve success in life and enjoy happiness.

Beyond a mere philosophy, STOICISM is also a lifestyle. If you pursue the route of "freedom by reason and passion," then you will be able to endure the challenges of life. You'll be prepared to face every curveball life throws at you.

Do you think of yourself as an adherent of this idea? Only one method to know and that's by studying the subject. Stoicism represents as a thought-form. So, whether Gen Z or not It appears that it's back into school...

What was the date when Stoicism begin?

If you're bored in the subject of history choose an alternative route. Continue towards the next page and discover what you can do to be "free from the lust for life."

As a philosophical concept, STOICISM originated in ancient Greece about 300 B.C. It was taught first through an old Greek philosopher called Zeno of Citium who later developed the concept as a refinement of a philosophy we're aware by the name of CYNICISM. So, Cynicism and Stoicism may appear to you as the same way however they are two distinct things. At first, one should avoid thinking that being Stoic similarly means to be an Cynic.

At the time the concept of Cynicism was thought of as a rogue. When it came to finding inner virtue and striving for higher morality its adherents would often challenge the norms of society. They sought to serve the greater good and refused to be ruled by. This is quite a contrast from the idea of a Cynic nowadays and is typically described as self-centered, self-centered and indifferent.

Through its modernization, Stoicism integrated ASCETICISM as an exercise. In the past, it signified a person's choice to abstain from the world's ways. The person chose to stay away from the material, worldly pleasures of the world. As an individual who sought the higher level of spiritual goals , not just one that was material, an Ascetic engaged in self-denial. Through this they made a decision to live an unassuming and sacrificial life that was geared towards the virtues.

Zeno himself was succeeded by a successor whose name was Cleanthes Assos. Then, as an apprentice and follower of Cleanthes it is Chrysippus who was a student of Soli who was instrumental in spreading an influence from the philosophy that we are now able to call Stoicism. At the time, Stoicism embodied the elements of ethics, logic, reasoning as well as physics today, they are unified.

The growth of Stoic ideas led to it being the most influential philosophy in the early days of Greece. Explore the Greco-Roman ancient world of Stoicism , and it would be the source of the most famous philosophers who were Panaetius as well as Posidinius, Cato and Epictetus, Seneca, and Marcus Aurelius.

If you dig further into the lives as well as the times Cato, Epictetus, Seneca as well as Marcus Aurelius, you'll discover that they are among some of the leading Stoics of their day. They're examples of ancients who's beliefs and practices can be relevant to the present.

What are the Philosophers Have to Say?

If you don't have any interest at all in philosophical topics Then shift your focus towards the following chapter. However, if you remain on this page, you'll start to learn about the various philosophical theories that led to the development of Stoicism.

If we could return to the past and discover how this philosophy was born in the first place, we could begin by defining it as a thought-process. Stoic thought was initially studied and then applied to the following concepts:

1. MONISM

Beginning at Monism, Stoic philosophers agree that all is one. In particular, there is only one divine reality in the entire, vast universe.

While this body is one It has many parts that are connected. We all are part of the same whole.

Since we all are connected and a part of the totality, what is affecting one, will also affect the other.

The most committed Monists claim that our destiny has been set in stone. While we are guided by our choice, however we are guided by a higher motive that leads us towards the divine.

2. MATERIALISM

In accordance to Materialism, Stoic philosophers propose that the universe is made of material. Our body is a material. Our words , and even our emotions are made of material.

We should think about Metaphysics However, it is possible to conclude that the universe is material and the ether. There is the material and passive side of the universe. Additionally, there is the active, ethereal aspect of it, which is more sophisticated and has greater reasoning. This is where the soul of the human is born, and is sometimes referred to as"the "primordial flame." Philosophers also refer to it as "fate" and "logos."

3. EUDAEMONISM

There are two versions of Eudaemonism The modern perspective and an older one. The more ancient version states that there exists a series of events that will happen throughout your life. Even though you have the freedom to choose however, your choice of actions is formed according to the circumstances.

Today there are numerous debates over whether or not we're the ones who decide our fate and what the reason. Is fate the determining factor in our lives or does our free choice determine the direction that we live our lives? In the case of the ancient Stoics They believed in the power of Zeus and believed in the divine providence.

With a modernized idea, Eudaemonism says that you can be successful in your life and be content regardless of your efforts to be the best you can be. One of the ways you let goodwill to be the dominant force is to are at peace with the natural world as well as with other people. This is possible through your capability to be able to think and reason.

As a distinct Eudaemonistic concept, Stoicism believes in an end-to-end aim for all human endeavours. This is also known as Eudaemonia. Since it refers to an attitude of bliss and happiness anyone would consider it worthwhile to pursue.

This is the time to call everyone Gen Z and Gen Z lovers all over the world: Wouldn't you wish to feel at peace with a new outlook? Wouldn't you like to see your family and friends prospering in their lives? Stoics affirm that this could happen right here and present, if you are practicing Stoicism. It is beneficial when you let yourself put aside the practice of reliving the past instead, you live now in this moment.

If yes you're in, then there's no reason to be hesitant about taking a look at the theory. As educated as you are at the age of your life and at this phase of the course of your existence, you're likely to gain more knowledge through this particular school of thinking. Consider it!

What is its relationship to other ideologies?

If, on the other hand, you're not a fan of tea to talk about matters of religion and beliefs, then it's the best time to skip this part and go straight to the next chapter.

However in the event that you are from the generation which is open to religious and racial diversities, we'd not hesitate to talk about certain similarities with your generation. Indeed, the Stoicism's philosophy Stoicism has many ideas in common with other ideologies and religions like Buddhism, Islam, and Christianity.

1. STOICISM and BUDDHISM

The four primary TRUTHS that an Buddhist adheres to, and they correspond to principles that the Stoic holds to. They are:

A) Life is not without suffering and that it is a normal part of the human condition.

B) This suffering is the result of the desires and passions of one's.

C) This the freedom from your passions will bring you happiness.

d) The possibility of being free of suffering if you practice self-control and attain moral control.

2. ISLAM AND STOICISM

In the same vein as SUFFERING Both believe in a higher cause in which people aren't given an burden they are unable to take on. They believe that we are able in us as individuals to face every challenge and face the trials of life.

As a way to live as a way of life, both Stoicism and Islam inspire their followers to strive to lead a happy life. While being in harmony with others and being in tune with nature. The life of a person should be devoted to living in harmony with nature. That's right being in tune with it, and not in opposition to it.

3. STOICISM AS WELL AS CHRISTIANITY

As an ideal way of living Both Stoicism and Christianity require you to apply Virtue in your everyday life. One example of the shared virtues is to be kind to your neighbors and to be a servant to your fellow citizens.

They both believe in the control over the WILL. You can make yourself a promise to be a good person and be a good person. In the face of the difficulties of life, you have to accept these challenges and let the higher power to triumph.

As an aside, Stoicism received a major revolution in the Renaissance time. It was historically, the time when people witnessed the rise of Neo-Stoicism. As an ideology, Neo-Stoicism was well-known among its Christian population. The reason for this was that the concept was made more acceptable to Christians because of the conviction that one should surrender the will of God and not be influenced by emotions. There were four primary passions listed, and they included sorrow, joy, fear, and greed.

Here's the main point: Regardless of what your beliefs may be or what kind of ideology you adhere to, we're not different from one another. Particularly, for those belonging to Generation Z, you're now more open to a different sort of world.

It's really not our differences that distinguish us, but our commonalities that connect us. When you have Stoicism at work, we aware that, as different as we may be, we have many things that we have in the same.

Everyone has their own fair share of difficulties in our lives. Everyone wants to be free of pain and all of us want to be happy. Everyone must work with nature and work at peace with one another. It is possible when we all strive for the greater GOOD and attain the aim of MODERATION in our lives.

Chapter 13: Learn What Passion Is

If you're a member of the Z generation, you'll avoid being passionate about things that instantly satisfy. You can get the things you desire in a flash. Whatever you want can be found in only two clicks. It's instant gratification facilitated through the Internet!

Unfortunately, this need for instantaneous and immediate is a powerful force for people. These desires not only keep you from doing your work, they also deceive you. It is easy to give to your emotions rather than using your mind. That's the problem with Generation Z, along with previous generations.

The issue isn't that it is unsolvable or that the people aren't able to change. It's more of finding a solution that can be effective. You'll find out more in Part 2 STOICISM can be the solution. With LOGIC and REASON it is possible to achieve an end to obsession.

What is Passion Defined?

In everyday the language of everyday life, PASSION means an extreme emotion. As intense as the emotion might be it is, it can be destructive, and even more so if the individual does not possess the motivation or capability for it to be transformed into more beneficial good.

We shouldn't be able to say but we can say that none of your desires are bad and every one of them is bad. It's actually your unstable, unruly feelings that turn into self-destructive ones. If you are overcome by them then you lose your control.

In daily life In everyday life, it's when you let your emotions take over your thinking that you lose respect for yourself and forget about the results from your choices. Naturally the actions you take will have consequences that could be short-term or long-term. Consider anger, which can cause violence and conflict, for example.

It is evident that this is distinct from your love of music or sports, which are beneficial and healthy. It is also important to be distinguished from everyday desires, lusts and desires.

A desire is a strong sense of desire. The desire is intense and can drive you insane. This desire may be directed at an individual (a individual) or towards something (an object or outcome). There is pleasure in the concept of something, and excitement about the idea of someone.

Be aware that desire and longing may not always translate into action. If you have a desire however, you might or may not be able to act upon it.

Let LUST be your guide. Lust is among our most intense desires, and it can overwhelm us. It can be so intense that it can cause you to lose control. So, you can find things as lust for sexual sex and money and an obsession with power.

When you say WHIM it's an instantaneous and impulsive urge. A bit of a wild idea and it could even be unintentional.

In the age that is Gen Z where everything is immediate and spontaneous, impulses are easy to give to. For instance what is the most often you embark on an excursion without thinking about it? What happens when we make purchases hundreds of items with one swipe of a credit card?

It's important to remember it's not just about OBSESSIONS as well. "Being obsessed" is a phrase we love to talk about nowadays. We often say that we're obsessed with our clothes or the celebrities we love. We make the point that people are obsessed with cleanliness and order. Certain of these terms are incorrect, and we must clarify what is an obsession.

Do not mistake an obsession with an emotion; it's an idea. It's an idea that is constantly occupying your thoughts. Since there is a disturbance and tension.

As they become more stressful obsessive thoughts could be detrimental to you. They're persistent and can be time-consuming. They encroach on your daily routine at times when you require rest and recovery. In a state of sleeplessness and restlessness is when it is easy to cave into the urge. Most often, the compulsion is a result of something that is psychologically harmful and emotionally damaging.

Because of this (or for no the reason) It happens that you follow someone, or someone you stalk. They bully you or intimidate you online.

There are many events that can occur because of intense lusts, desires and desires which is the reason you must control your desires. It can be done by being aware of your thoughts and managing your emotions as a more emotionally-intelligent person.

What does Apathy mean?

In other words, let us assist you in understanding what ancient Greeks were referring to by Apathy. The word"PASSION" comes from the Greek word pathos. It is a term used to describe suffering related to emotions or feelings. To conquer this kind of discomfort, Stoics insist that you should not just utilize your intellect and logic but also employ apathy.

The term "apathy" is one that is associated with our current world. In the present, when people are becoming aloof towards each other and unresponsive to the needs of others it is now translated into an absence of concern and interest. It's no longer meaningful.

If you really want to become a Stoic and agnostic, you need to know the meaning of Apatheia actually means. It's a passive reaction to external events that surround you. They are ignored in the sense that you believe that all of these events can be considered to be either positive or negative in their own way.

It is actually your own inner self that can become constructive or destructive. When we speak of the "INNER SELF," we are talking about your thoughts and feelings. They are in your.

When you practice apathy, you are able to eliminate the desires that reside in your. In the old world they were described as a fluttering in the soul. Also known as ptoia, they are felt as tension or disturbance.

In the present From a Stoic's perspective these desires are emotions that are not rational. They are not governed by the rules of logic or reasoning. An obsession can be so intense that it can reach the point of no return. Then, it can become destructive.

In addition More than that, Stoics are also able to recognize that Stoic is also a believer in a passion as a false notion. Because of a false belief that an impulse is generated. Ideally, one is supposed to remain in a state of passiveness and be indifferent to the stimuli. Then, judgement is made and the assent is accepted. In the end, one is triggered to react to the basis of an argument or insult such as. In worst cases it can be a chaotic situation.

What are the reasons to let go of your passion?

With all the fire that extreme passions can cause it is clear that we must to be free of them. It is crucial, perhaps vital, to be free of passion due to the five primary reasons listed below. Without wasting time Here's the WHY:

1. Passions are unrational.

As we've mentioned that they are clearly defying any logic or reason. However, as frenzied as they can be and a dangerous thing to do is mix the extreme emotions along with obsessional thoughts.

2. Passions are inconsiderate.

As extravagant as they may be however, they can also be outrageous. They can thwart your ultimate purpose of living a healthy lifestyle. From being simple, they can transform your life into one that's difficult. They disrupt your inner peace of peace and create anxiety in you.

3. The passions of people may be incorrect.

They are usually the result from false beliefs. They are derived from rapid judgements. As wolves They've been fed over long periods of time and with preconceived beliefs.

So, pay attention to Gen Z because we've got an answer! The answer is to control these emotions today and stop allowing them to rule the day. You can feed these feelings by taking a smaller amount in your thinking. They will get very little of your time or energy. Keep an eye on these old bad behaviors weaken and will disappear with the course of. That's how you train yourself to get rid of all your prejudices and biases.

4. Passions can be powerful.

It was Chrysippus who best explained the runaway obsession. It's like who is running downhill but and not being able to stop. If you're unable to stop yourself without a reason The strength of your desire grows. The sheer force pushes you to move forward. As the momentum grows it becomes becoming increasingly difficult to stop. This is why it's important to put your brakes in place to stop angry drivers.

5. Passions are bodily.

They are a manifestation of your body. The skin flushes and the blood boils when you're stressed. Your skin is pale and your pulse flutters when you're afraid. Your heart hurts and suffers when you're in a state of distress. Whatever your passions in life and they will manifest. They will be felt in the physical sense.

Now, we understand why it is crucial to be free of our passions and that is why we need to do it. This is the only way to be free of our false perceptions and negative thoughts about others. This is the only way to stay clear of arguments, misinterpretations and conflicts that can result in conflict and war. All of them are an end to suffering.

To avoid these emotions from growing unnoticed Also, it is essential to acknowledge these feelings as they really are. They are irrational, false as well as abrasive and uncontrollable. Yet, since they are a part of the body it is possible to feel passions physically as they occur. This means you will not be "unfeeling" in the way that the majority of people think.

Chapter 14: Achieve Freedom From Passion

What is it that it means to be completely free from passion? Is it a signification of being emotionally detached and indifferent? Are you indifferent and uncaring? Are you apathetic and indifferent to anyone?

In the previous chapter, we've learned that being Stoic does not mean you're indifferent. In fact it is possible to feel the beginning of a passion , and the signs of it show within your body.

Furthermore, if being Stoic is to not feel and unfeeling, it's not painting any kind of picture of people of the Next Generation. If this were the case and it was to become a viral phenomenon and spread across the world, then our existence is just an unfeeling zombie.

There has to be more than "freedom of passion" to allow Stoics to have remained with the concept for so long. If FREEDOM FROM PAIN and SUFFERING is the prize that is being sought, then the pursuit of it is truly worthwhile. If suffering is all-encompassing, what advantage that would bring!

What are the four passions you Have to Manage?

With CONTROL being the main word and CONTROL being the key word, it's clear that you need to begin getting rid of these passions. You must establish more control over your own self to free yourself from any unfounded, insanity-inducing powerful, and unmoderate obsessions.

Once we understand how these passions influence us, we need to determine what should not be affecting us. There are four major passions that have been identified These are the things Stoics attempt to stay at ease with:

1. DISTRESS

Have you ever been such a sense of anxiety over someone or something else that it brought you grief and sorrow? The younger generations are referred to as ANGST However, this is the thing that Stoics describe as DISTRESS.

For instance in the case of Gen Z readers, you may still feel lonely despite forming groups.

Sure, you've got many friends and the connections seem to be present however, you are still feeling lonely. The feeling of being unconnected and alone can be very troubling.

Stress can be better described as an internal condition of tension and tenseness. Accept the stress of your emotions and it won't disappear but will keep increasing. It could get worse until it alters your thoughts and influences your behaviour.

2. Fear

Are you scared of falling short? Do you often worry that you may not be successful at something, or be a failure to someone? Are you scared of not being valued or being disregarded?

Naturally, fear is a huge disappointment. Fear of falling down to others. You're also afraid that other people might disappoint you. Therefore, you are losing your love and relationships particularly when these worries are not true.

In terms of what fear actually is, it's the overwhelming feeling that something or someone will turn out to be harmful or even dangerous to you. The feeling of fear is usually generated through triggers. Therefore, anxiety can be caused and provoked by a myriad of causes, some which are: FRUSTRATION REJECTION, FAILURE and lastly the UNKNOWN.

If any of these aspects make you feel uncomfortable and you're scared, you must get rid of the habit of being scared. Instead, you must be able to conquer your fear. Although it's not an easy feat, but certainly not impossible to achieve The first step is to face your fears. Only when you are able to recognize and comprehend your fears that you will be capable of controlling your fears.

3. LUST

We've discussed LUST before as an extreme sense of desire. It could be a craving for power, sex and wealth as well as possessions. Even though the actual battle with it is difficult, removing yourself from desire is achievable.

It's the matter of making a decision to take or not take action. Sure, the object of your desire could be in the room and the presentation might be excellent. However, the most important aspect is to not be attracted to its appeal and get away from the root of the attraction.

Although it's not as easy as it sounds it is possible to distract yourself and divert your focus by doing the simplest tasks. In reality, it's an issue of making sure your mind is occupied to ensure that your mind takes over. Since it is what happens to your brain's structure, it will.

If you're tempted to have a play with the waitress, for instance or while for a night out with your friend, switch your attention at the menu. Concentrate on something else that is competing with your images - for instance, the small letters that explain what you'll get as well as the little information about how it's going to be cooked. This could cause boredom to those who are Gen Z in you, but that's not the point.

As soon as you've had the sensation in reading, and trying to understand your brain's process. As distracted as you may have been you were, it might or might not grasp, but at minimum, you've made progress. The immediate urge is gone and you've likely slowed the pace just in time to enjoy a wonderful meal.

4. DELIGHT

When it comes to DELIGHT The word can be applied in many ways. It is possible to be thrilled with your pet's adorable and hilarious actions. Your friend will be thrilled with a gift or visit from your. If you succeed in this regard the event, your partner could be thrilled that you had a wonderful night out without any fuss.

The pleasure that Stoics are referring to is more than that. It's a genuinely pleasurable experience that causes you to long and desire. The cause of pleasure takes all of your attention however, the satisfaction you feel from it doesn't last long. So, you're stuck between experiencing the joy and wanting more.

Additionally, it manifests as the desire to thrill. The experiences you have aren't satisfying enough, so you're always looking for the next experience that will be your best. Insane about the cost and the risk it is always necessary to stay "out out there." The desire never ends.

Where do these passions take to

Because passions can be overpowering and all-consuming and consuming, they can be hard to control. They can cycle and take you on a loop and lead you to nowhere. It's pleasure after pleasure, anxiety feeding fear, lust building another desire, and so on.

It's clear that there's nothing innocent in these desires. It's early to realize and accept that these passions can be harmful and destructive! Each one of us will examine what they do to you and the direction they take:

1. It's DISTRESS which can cause a lot of angst to your soul. Most often because of anger and discontent with your life, it can trigger feelings of jealousy, anger and resentment toward your neighbour. They can cause a breakdown in relationships because you want what they clearly possess and also what you do not.

This can also cause feelings of anxiety, worry as well as feelings of anguish, frustration, and discontent at your self. If you are unhappy and dissatisfied with the person is you, can lose confidence in yourself. It is possible to lash out at your family and friends, or the world at large.

2. Being the way that it truly is can lead to the worst feeling that something negative will happen. You fear for your life. You fear losing your property. You think you're greedy and selfish because you're fearful of losing it. These worries can be described as DREAMS.

Particularly if you're superstitious, your fear of the unknown could fool you. If you're overcome by fear, you are frightened, panicked and terror even when you encounter the most insignificant, significant of events.

In the case of anxiety about failure and rejection it can result in anxiety and personal pain. Unloved and feeling unworthy can cause people to take their own lives to the point of becoming suicide. This is the reason suicides take place.

3. In its own way LUST is an appetite that jumbles your brain. Particularly, when the lust is sexual, you send and receive multiple signals. Insatiably satisfied either with yourself or the otherperson, you feel anguish,

hunger as well as rage and self-loathing simultaneously.

Furthermore, your desire can destroy relationships with others. This can lead you to commit infidelities and sexy acts which cause more suffering and pain for those who care about you as well as the loved ones you cherish. This is self-defeating.

4. Don't be fooled into thinking that there is nothing wrong regarding DELIGHT at all. Since it's all about immediate self-gratification, this is likely to be one of the biggest issues that Gen Z faces.

In the event that the need to feel happy becomes routine, the thrill fades away. It is easy to become dissatisfied with the source of your previous happiness. But, you're still dependent on it, and you feel depressed in the absence of it.

For instance, take your smartphone. When you first purchase one, you're happy. A new model comes out and you're looking for another and another. You're never satisfied until you're on par with your friends, and that can be both expensive and tiring.

If these powerful emotions can be a part of your life that you relate to and can relate to, then Stoicism is the right medicine for you! You shouldn't be a slave to the emotions of lust and pleasure. Similar to an illness that disables you, you shouldn't be restrained by fear and stress.

In the end you'll need to stabilize your emotions. If not, you'll end up in a rollercoaster of emotions for a lifetime. It's a long time to be in to use, but take a look what the human race has been from the past to the present.

The most difficult part is that a lot of these negative emotions are self-inflicted. They make you suffer but you accept them to continue. As you old age (and in any other age) there is a massive cost to pay for when they cause depression.

Are you ready to be Free of Passion?

If this is the rollercoaster of emotions that has marked many the time during your teenage days then the answer should be an affirmative YES! Aren't there a reason you aren't willing to say that you're ready to live completely free of all emotions? It's time to do it.

If you're just ready to leave the train, this is the time to stop. We're not saying you should give up on your beliefs. We're also not encouraging you to stop having love for the things that you cherish.

What we're revealing to you right now Generation Z is that you're not yet to discover what it means to be Passion-free. What exactly does Stoics refer to as having no passion? From the perspective of a Stoic's point of view, let's learn what it means and not.

1. The definition of freedom from passion is not an absence of emotion, nor the absence of emotion. It doesn't mean you must be emotionless.

2. To be uninvolved in your passion doesn't mean that you will be emotionally indifferent, neither. Living, intelligent, and vibrant being which you're, weren't intended to be so boring.

3. A person who is not afflicted from passion isn't concerned and caring. While it's the fact that Stoics are often ridiculed and accused of being indifferent and uncaring, it isn't what a genuine Stoic is. As Stoics, you are not indifferent to anything. Stoic you're not apathetic solely to all four deep passions listed in the sense that they impact you and cause you to make mistakes.

4. Let's see what FREEDOM from PASSION is about:

A) It's about not giving in to those desires (or excessive desires) which fuel the desire (or intense thoughts). The goal you set for yourself and others is a solitary life free from suffering.

B) It's about overcoming every emotion whether positive or negative. The positive within you can be resilient and triumph regardless of the situation.

C) It's about controlling your emotions and controlling your emotions and regulating them. As you control emotion, you are able to keep your emotions under control.

d) It is about forming an improved response to the various situations that you face. This means that your emotional response is more appropriate.

e) In addition to creating a rational response to all things, it's about responding in an ethical manner. The reason for this is that Stoicism can be described as more than just a rational philosophical system. Through time it was always meant as an ethics system.

Chapter 15: Be Aware Of Your Stoic Virtues

And Emotions

We concluded the previous chapter by stating that STOICISM is moral as well as ethical. As a principle it firmly believes that man must be in harmony with all things. Man is at liberty to exercise his own will. However, any exercise that enhance his health only when it is in harmony with nature and the environment.

What's going to be gained in reading this chapter? The reason is that if you have a good understanding of the emotions and virtues of Stoics, Stoic theorist, you will discover how to manage emotion and enjoy with peace and harmony.

If you are part of Generation Z, what are your personal views about the current world? Are there areas where you believe our morality could be improved, and how can we improve our morality? What are the steps you've taken since you mastered your own feelings?

3. Stoic Emotions to develop

Are you aware of the feelings that can lead you to an attitude in which you feel "all well"? This state of blissful and thriving is called Eupatheia. In addition to Apatheia (in where you were completely indifferent and indifferent to events outside) You moved toward being happy.

What feelings are there that might be able to be able to replace your most unruly desires? It's likely that you'll be shocked to find out that they're not so complicated as you'd like to believe. The 3 powerful emotions you'll need to master are as easy and common as:

1. Joy

While pleasure is inaccessible, it is happiness that is more enduring. The pleasures of life are fleeting and infrequent but the pleasures of living (along with the pleasures of nature) are the most long-lasting and last for a long time.

JOY can be described as an emotion that is felt. The feeling of elation is both rational and sensible. You can be content with the things you own, it is also a sense of peace and tranquility in your character.

In the end the definition of happiness is yours to choose. You have the power to decide the level of happiness you want to be.

Your own inner happiness tells you that even if it's not possible to acquire all the possessions that are material and enjoyments, you can still be content. It's possible to be happy even in the most basic things.

In contrast to pleasures that often need to be pursued, joy isn't a requirement to pursue. It's just a matter of finding it within yourself. Only the pursuit of VIRTUE is worthwhile since it is the highest quality.

2. WISH

From our own desires for pleasure Sometimes, we long for things that aren't ours. We are prone to cravings and desire things belonging to other people.

Instead of allowing this urge, it's best to cultivate a desire. Wishing means actively striving towards the target. If the goal is achieved or not, you're fulfilled and content. Since there is acceptance and acceptance, you can show kindness and compassion. You don't suffer, and you don't cause others to suffer.

3. CAUTION

Be aware it is an unintentional abstention from something that you believe to be risky or even dangerous. While there is no evidence for this conclusion however, you believe it as a threat or threat.

In contrast to fear there is the rational abstention from something which clearly has the potential for harm. Since it is rational and sensible This is called AVOIDANCE.

There's a vast distinction between being suspicious of your surroundings and becoming aware. Being wary is a feeling of fear and sceptical. The awareness comes from being aware of the reality. Your senses are active. In the absence of a intention for recklessness, move cautiously!

4. Stoic Virtues Fit for Gen Z

In general the term "virtue" refers to an ideal moral state. Since one is virtuous the person is naturally prone to conduct well. In the individual, virtues are characteristics or traits that an individual is blessed with, and are considered to be desirable and morally right.

The act of doing good leads to excellence, not just as an individual (individually) however, as group (collectively). Inability or lack of virtue however often leads to VICE.

When we use the term "ethical," we refer to both good and bad actions. ETHICS is a set of principles that are aligned with morality. These principles are based upon virtues that are considered morally acceptable.

There are many virtues that provide the basis for moral behavior, Stoics uphold FOUR CARDINAL Virtues in particular. These are:

1. WISDOM

Do you remember how to abandon your foolish habits as you age? This, in part is WISDOM. Sophia in Greek is the capacity to think with reasoning based on knowledge and experiences.

Additionally, Wisdom means gaining a more thorough understanding of human experience is not just for you, but also for the perspective of other people. Since you are aware and awake that you can be aware, think, and act accordingly.

There are certain characteristics connected with being wise and they include:

a) Intelligence. Not only are you intelligent, you're also alert and sharp. The relaxed aspect of you may be funny and witty. Are you a smart person with a ability to laugh?

b) Resourcefulness. Do you consider resourcefulness to be among your top strengths? Being resourceful implies that you can solve problems and find an answer, even with limit of resources.

c) Sensibility. Are your decisions rational and sound? If you use your sense when making a decision you're more likely to be successful and less likely to make a mistake in your judgment.

d) Risk assessment. Are you thinking before you take action? Are your decisions calculated well? Don't let us fool you If you're in this situation the term "calculating" doesn't necessarily mean making plans on how to make money. Instead, it's about understanding the implications and deciding on the most effective option.

e) Discreetness. A person with discretion dress and behaves in a manner that's respectful of other people. They are in a position to keep information from being shared that is not appropriate to share, just because it's too personal or valuable to other people. How is your privacy?

f) Tact. With discretion comes tactfulness. You're able to monitor your words and act in a manner that doesn't cause the risk of offense. You don't want to cause or be involved in conflicts which is evident through your conduct. Are you respectful towards others or are you apathetic?

2. COURAGE

COURAGE Courage, also known as Andreia in Greek is about being robust. It is also about knowing what must be done when difficulties arise. Instead of being scared and timid, you can find it within you to be courageous!

People who are courageous have the following traits:

a) Endurance. If you're a patient, enduring person? It's not just about waiting around for an application to be loaded... The word endurance means being able to endure any kind of hardship regardless of the length of the wait or how painful the experience. It's a must-have trait in these times of uncertainty.

b) Resilience. Anyone who perseveres grows resilient. The person who endures accepts the circumstance and this permits them to bounce back and recuperate. Are you able to handle the challenges at work, with your partner or at school?

c) Industriousness. How committed are you to your studies as well as other tasks? If you think that work is valuable and that it's beneficial to be a hard worker If so, then you're on right path.

d) Principle. Do you do what's right? Are you adamant without feeling self-righteous? If you are a person of principle You set up clear and precise ideals that are worthy of pursuit. It is your ethical and moral principles to define you as a person.

3. JUSTICE

JUSTICE Justice, or Dikaiosyne in Greek is the act of doing things correctly and with fairness to other people. Fairly-minded people are able to interact not only with their fellows as well as with people from different levels. They are transparent of their actions, either at home or in public.

The sense you have of justice manifests itself in various ways:

a) Honesty. Do you have the desire to be honest? The top priority on our list, honesty goes with a righteous mindset. It's part of the moral fabric that defines your character.

b) Fairness. Do you make an effort to live your life and fight fair? Fairness lets you practice the right and honest treatment for other people, whether in your work or intimate relationships. Through being fair, you'll be free of bias and prejudice.

Chapter 16: Generation Z On Time Management

According to a study that found According to the study, 70% of student believe that their school needs to be re-examined and rethink its approach to digital technology. The realities of students who are digital shows that 79 percent of Generation Z consumers show signs of distress and emotional stress when they are away from their devices. Millenials struggle with dealing with or understanding the digital world of Generation Z. Statistics can demonstrate that by showing that while Millenials utilize three screens per day, Gen Z uses five devices: a TV, smartphone and laptop, a desktop computer, and music players. The impact of digitalization on school institutions shows how 36% students think that they do not spend as much time studying because administration is difficult and 47% believe that student administration to be simpler to manage due to the high costs they have to pay as well as 41% of students stated that they'd have an improved experience when they were able to interact more electronically with their school. The results also show an assessment of how simple the students find it to manage various aspects of their lives in the digital age. Rankings show:

1. Online Shopping

Today's youth, particularly Generation Z, find the pleasure of looking through the thousands of merchandise on the internet. Gen Z find it easy to dedicate time to online shopping as it is also regarded as therapeutic, drawing your attention to all the things you can purchase with one click. According to a study from 2011 released within The Journal of Psychology and Marketing shopping has tremendous positive effects in your overall mood. The study revealed the fact that 28% shoppers bought something to commemorate some event or personal win and 62% of them bought something to cheer their spirits. The study shows that money is a great way to purchase happiness.

2. Entertainment/Music

There is no doubt that the majority of people find it more pleasant and easier to do work when there's music. Similar to that the majority of people feel more relaxed and relieves stress when having fun. In the case of Gen Z, entertainment is an opportunity to relax after a long or tiring day. It is also the top priority by the majority of students due in a lack of motivation to complete schoolwork and prefer to relax with films and games or browsing on social networks. Music is, however helps to ease stress of stressful situations, or relaxing. Music is also an effective method of dealing with feelings, based on your mood.

3. Social media/Social Life

Gen Z finds it very simple to control their time on social media. Social media can also be a method of entertainment, where one can post images or videos to social media for the entire World Wide Web to see. Social media can be utilized in a variety of ways, including creating awareness, making a person "viral" and famous or famous, signing petitions, giving to groups, or simply displaying a portion of one's daily life on the lens of a screen. For Generation Z being on the go, staying up to date with their social media is essential. Many Gen Z find it difficult to get through their day without a smartphone in their pocket or without checking their social media accounts every time. Social media is now an integral segment in Generation Z, which is why being able to meet their needs digitally could have a beneficial impact.

4. Finances/Banking

Making deposits, investing or moving money can be accomplished via the internet. Not having to visit the bank is long gone, and now it is possible to manage one's finances in a single click. This is a great opportunity for Gen Z made use of this advantage and utilized it in their daily lives to track their earnings or savings online. Gen Z find this extremely beneficial as they don't need to leave the comforts of their home to handle their financial affairs. It's also very practical especially for Gen Z who work online or do freelance work, as they can track their earnings simply by looking at the tiny display of a smartphone tablet or computer.

5. Travel

The many options of places to travel can be done digitally too. A visit to a website where it reviews specific places that one would like to visit has resulted in a much more efficient way of looking through options. Looking into what you could purchase for the specific budget for your trip, what activities you can take part in, and the destinations you can visit are advertised on the Internet. Exploring digitally gives you the sensation like you are in the location you are in, as well as a digital representation of the landmarks of the location and the people who make one feel as if they were in the exact place.

6. University Life

Some institutions haven't been digitally savvy, which makes it difficult for students to communicate with their administration. In the end that it's considered to be as one of the lowest of a student's concerns due to the lack of professionalism and routine of professional support online. Apart from the small to adapt students would prefer things other than participate in activity that is related to school. In today's digital age there are a myriad of things that students could be drawn to, but the distractions keep students from taking part in college life on the internet. This is a sign that schools and schools should be able to be able to adapt to Generation Z's requirements to make more impact on the individual.

What do students really would they like?

One quarter of respondents feel they are less satisfied with their school due to their poor systems 41% of students are inclined to suggest their school when digital interactions were better and 33% of students believe there's too much paperwork and work to be completed and get annoyed by the volume and the complexity of administration. Students are not as satisfied with these aspects:

1. Managing Financial Aid

2. Transfer of Courses

3. Communication with Advisors to Faculty

4. Controlling the Academic Progression and Coursework

5. The cost of tuition

6. Admissions

Statistics reveal that 87% of college students would like an app or web app that is that can be accessed from any device. They are more content when their school established a single system for managing the entire administration. Eight of ten students find it beneficial to have an app that demonstrates the progress they are making in their studies.

Ideas for Thinking Strategies Generation Z

It is a fantastic opportunity to ahead of adjusting to the requirements that are expected of Gen Z digitally, when everything is planned. Here are a few suggestions to set up your thinking methods that are suitable for Gen Z:

1. Make sure to think digitally in all assignments, assessments, and other activities

When it comes to schoolwork students can get bored and lose interest when they look at an empty sheet of paper, waiting for ideas and thoughts to stimulate their minds with imagination. Start considering on letting them engage in digital activities. Allow them to watch a movie or a brief documentary, or upload a photo or video based on the subject or other subject that has students engaging in digital tasks. Students are more attentive and engaged in the work at task when they are doing it digitally. They find it easier for them to work by typing, clicking, or looking at something via their computer screens. Digital learning is an excellent method for students to learn as the digital world is a regular element of their lives. In a digital world they feel comfortable and are more engaged in, it will enhance the motivation and interest of students in their schoolwork. Notify students of forthcoming homework assignments that have deadlines close to due to assist them in managing their time. Students are more likely to overlook forthcoming assignments because the assignments are all online, and deadlines are often close, particularly when school projects have different subjects.

2. Break content into short segments

Teaching students using digital methods can get boring for them, particularly when lessons and modules are incredibly long and monotonous. To keep them interested and awake, it's recommended to cut lessons into smaller pieces and make it more engaging by adding videos, jokes or any other form of entertainment that could be linked to the subject. In the classroom setting it is also advisable to include interesting facts or trivia between lessons, or even make stories that students are able to understand. In addition, providing entertainment for students in class will help students remember what they learned while keeping them entertained and engaged by the subject. It also allows students to be more eager to attend classes as they are aware that it provides entertainment and fun while they get to discover new things each day. Relying on the lesson plan by itself with no added "color" or some creativity the subject can be boring for students, but teachers too. Teachers are now educating Gen Z and their parents, it is essential to change their methods of teaching to a style that students are familiar with instead of sticking using the same old methods of teaching are followed, result in students becoming bored and exhausted mentally.

3. Create information in a graphic and bite-sized

It is also essential to include visuals and images when instructing Gen Z. Through this, students are more involved in the subject and absorb information more effectively. Visuals can make the lessons easier to comprehend as they provide illustrations or examples visually, rather than just focusing on explanations, words and formulas by themselves. Graphics will not only aid students in understanding the subject better and provide the impression about "realness". Many teachers recognize the value of using visual aids or graphics to help students get grasp of the topic. Teachers appreciate the help that visual aids can provide to the classroom teaching because they can help students to establish a connection between the various pieces of information and absorb small amounts of content quickly and serve as memory aids. Making the content small and bite-sized aids students in understanding the subject better because it doesn't force them to absorb a large amount of language that could be boring and draining as each module is read. It is best to give students brief, concise information instead of pages of lectures, but the subject matter is irrelevant. Given that Gen Z having short attention span due to the constant exposure of other electronic devices making the information concise will allow each student to comprehend the lesson better.

4. Think about how you can communicate

Communication is essential, particularly when dealing with students that are part of Generation Z. The most efficient and simple method to improve the behavior of students is through constructive and effective communication. Communication is quite complex and can be utilized to deter negative behavior, promote good behavior, and boost positive behavior. A teacher's proximity to a pupil, the most subtle facial expression, the tiniest shift in voice or even the smallest of movements can signal an array of messages. Effective communication skills can be beneficial in both professional and personal life. While written and verbal skills for communication are still vital however, nonverbal behavior makes up an important portion of our everyday interactions with other people. Body language is vital too. It is thought of as an electronic transmitter, which is constantly transmitting signalling to brain. Teachers should be aware of these signals and know their effect on their students. If you need to correct the student behavior you can try slowing your body and dealing with misbehaviours in a formal , yet peaceful manner. This way students are likely to speak more freely and are more respectful instead of addressing the issue with anger and causing them to lash back. Gen Z is known to be very rebellious as well as sensitive, and it is essential to talk to students in a calm , approachable manner, like speaking to an acquaintance.

5. Be relevant. Be respectful of the time and needs that GenZ students have.

The majority of teachers love having students complete multiple school projects and some are to be completed on the same time. This can cause stress and exhaustion for students, given that they can't focus on one topic during a single day. In the case of Generation Z they are involved in a variety of activities beyond school, such as writing, sports or video blogging (video blogging) or any other form of entertainment that allows them to get away from the stress of school. Offering students multiple tasks isn't the best approach to teach them or be more engaged in the topic. Actually, it's hindering them from engaging in activities that will help them remain healthy and calm after school. Teachers must understand that students are likely to want to spend time off from school, or take part in things that aren't related to work at school. It's not healthy for students to be occupied with school work for every minute of their day without having time to pursue the things they enjoy, and getting very little or no time to rest. It is also observed that when students have sufficient time to relax and relax, especially when it's the time to get to a specific task, they tend to be more efficient and efficiently.

6. Give individual instruction - think of adaptive learning

Students benefit from active learning. Furthermore when properly implemented adaptive learning can make students more engaged. Teachers must plan the course to allow students to move easily through learning modules, practicing exercises and tests that allow them to improve their knowledge and build their abilities. It is important to ensure that the course incorporates active learning strategies like critical thinking, analysis, and knowledge creation. Use strategies to manage student ability to adapt. Incorporate socio-emotional and academic support for students who require it. After that, assess how it's effective.

Check if students are participating or are competent enough to reach more advanced levels of thought. Adaptive learning provides students with more practice and practice with the appropriate content and activities. When they are able to spend time on these activities, students are more involved. Implementing adaptive learning requires time and dedication and schools have to give teachers the resources and time, as well as credibility and acknowledgement. Schools must consider ways to assist teachers in a way that is effective. Teachers need time to develop new ways of learning. Schools must look at ways to alter the workload of faculty or tasks to free their time to develop an innovative and flexible learning experience for their students.

7. Make use of Social Media methods to learn

The main benefit for social networks is excellent and efficient communication. Students can interact to anyone at any time using apps like Messenger, WhatsApp, Viber and many more. Users can access these platforms via their mobile, tablet or laptop, and students can share questions, make video calls or phone calls. If students are struggling working on their assignments, they can effortlessly communicate with their classmates or teachers. They don't have to wait around and see the teacher in person. Social media helps students learn by assisting in sharing documents like via Google Drive Box, Google Docs and more. Some teachers also connect to their students via Google Meet, Zoom, and Facebook Live. It has been observed that students quickly become bored of writing and reading, however social media and the internet offer a variety of information on the internet that students are more interested in reading particularly if they are interesting and eye-catching animations. The benefits of education offered by social media sites are ones that allow students to engage in crucial lessons and master specific subjects with great efficiency. Social media websites provide most up-to-date information on a variety of topics in the school curriculum. With that students are given the chance to study and learn about what's current. Social media is like Wikipedia for students in the present. Generation Z is the era of learning through social media.

8. Help students prepare to be prepared for a future career

Engaging and fun activities to help students explore career possibilities is an excellent way to engage them in learning about the various careers they could pursue. Career-related activities can help students establish their goals in order that they are able to take the necessary steps to turn their dreams into reality. Finding the career exploration activities suitable for students may take some time however, it will benefit them tremendously in their future. Teachers may invite guests from various professions to share their experience with students. They are typically guests who have jobs which are familiar to students, to make it more exciting and motivating for the students. Discuss with students ways to achieve their career goals following high school. Assist them in identifying the steps they'll need to follow. Students may want to study the skills they'll require to master to become a part of for the specific course they wish to take. It is also important to know what qualifications for education and job requirements are required. Through this teachers are helping students broaden their perspectives about the various career options they could pursue in the near future. It can encourage them to offer them a wide range of choices. Making sure they know what skills will best fit their needs is a good method to guide them in the right path.

9. Access resources to assist in the elimination of student loan debt

The primary issue facing most students is their accumulated loans from students. According to hbr.org with a figure of nearly $1.6 trillion the student loan debt surpasses the amount of car loans accumulated and cards with credit. According to any standard this is a crisis it is definitely a problem for those who have student loan debts that have repayment schedules stretch over decades with massive monthly payments. Teachers can aid in the elimination of the student debts by giving students with sources and information that will assist them with their study. The most reliable educational resources require payment, and it's difficult for students to get the correct and precise details especially when they don't have any option to make additional purchases that could cost more than the savings they have each week. Don't be reluctant to give students tools that could be a significant impact on their school activities. Apart from offering the students with free resources, helping them to apply for grants and scholarships can be a wonderful method to assist them in reducing student debt. Aiding them to get the college scholarship is similar to providing them with free materials, in the form of a full curriculum and learning modules. In helping students discover ways of finding free funds for their education such as grants, discounts and scholarships is an effective method for decreasing the amount of student loans or eliminating debt.

10. Accept that the generation of today sees themselves as smart, creative and hardworking

As a teacher and an influencer that students admire and look up to, it is crucial for their development and mental well-being to inspire students and show them that they're doing a fantastic job. Every student has their own way of managing their mental health. They also have different capacities for how much information they absorb in a day. It is essential to let them know that they're enough and that they are making progress despite slow pace of progress. Give them praise for their creativity and dedication even if a few students have only were able to achieve half what the other students have achieved, tell them that they're doing a great job. A simple gesture of appreciation for their efforts can make a difference particularly when a student has been struggling with issues that they don't talk about. By showing them that their teacher values their well-being and admires them, they get an increased sense of inspiration and energy that pushes them to do great things within a short amount of seconds. Make them aware that their talents are unique and beautiful in its unique way, and they should continue to do what they are best at. Teachers can be their most trusted friend who they are at ease with and encourage them to be great while at the same time.

Generation Z on Careers and the Path to Success

A Study conducted in collaboration with Millenial Branding, a Generation Y research and consulting firm, as well as Randstad HR Services and staffing business, have stated the fact that Gen Z has an intelligible advantage over Gen Y because they are proven to have a more realistic outlook rather than optimistic, more likely to have a career outlook and adapt quickly to technological advances to be more effectively. The study also found that because Gen Z has seen the extent to which Gen Y has suffered during the recession, they go to work more equipped, less able and more qualified to be successful. Although the younger members of Gen Z Gen Z unit are still children and it's easy to overlook the work of researchers who have managed to squeeze millions of teenagers into a pattern of generational succession knowing the upcoming generation will be crucial for businesses and organizations that wish to be successful in the coming decade and beyond.

Accounting Principals conducted a study on the generational differences between Gen Z and Millennials. Gen Z in the workplace. A few of the major differences are:

1. Gen Z wants to change the world. 60 percent would like to make an impact on the world as compared to 39 percent of Millennials.

Gen Z was born in an age that exhibited the darkness and the cruelty that the entire world. Generation Z's elders generation have a strong desire to use their voices and platforms to stop the violence which millions suffer throughout the world due to various reasons. One of the issues that are extremely popular with all are their efforts in support of Black Lives Matter, giving an equal voice and rights in those in the LGBTQ+ community, registering to be able to vote in a responsible manner on elections for the next leaders of their nation and even making donations and petitions to organizations that aid in reducing the suffering of people all over the world. These are just the most important examples of how Gen Z has done in making a difference in the world. And so long as they're competent, this generation will continue to accomplish amazing and mind-opening activities that will make a huge influence on our world.

2. Gen Zers are multitasking across 5 screens or more per day and spend an average of 41 percent of their time away from school or work using mobile devices, compared with 22 percent Millennials 10 years ago.

Technology has advanced more as time has gone by. Since technology has become a regular element of a person's life, Gen Z has grown comfortable with having at least one or more devices within their reach. It's become aspect of their everyday lives and everything is easily accessible by using technology. Multitasking between Gen Z is quite common and includes screens that serve different functions. For instance, one screen is for a laptop or desktop, possibly for games or homework Another screen is used to be used as a mobile phone to send messages, a different screen for watching television, yet another screen to play music and the list goes on. In this type of environment, Gen Z tend to be more efficient and switch between screens without a problem.

3. One in two Gen Zers will have been educated at a University against 1 out of 4 Millennials

The importance of education has increased in each Gen Z individual. Gen Z are more likely to are driven to attending college following high school. select a course which will help them with their career path and then complete the course to be able to meet the necessary requirements for their chosen career. This is due to their desire for achieve a better life with great jobs, and due to that, the majority people in Gen Z want to study at a university and graduate from the school with an education.

4. Gen Z is 55 percent more likely to to start a business or employ others.

Gen Z is becoming more business-minded in comparison to Millenials and is aware of the benefits of what they will get when they begin small-scale enterprises. Gen Z has also seen and suffered through financial uncertainty, which is why they have the notion of starting businesses to ease the issue of not having enough money. In this way, it is now a source of inspiration for Gen Z to push through by pursuing a career in business and grow their business, thinking of this as a source of earning income in the future years. In addition, Gen Z has seen the benefits of starting small businesses particularly online, as everyone around the globe are more likely to do shop online instead of going to stores and other outlets in person. The internet has brought more than one could buy in a shopping mall. With that, Gen Z has grabbed the chance to be part of the online marketing business.

Conclusion

We've reached the final chapter of the book. Thanks for your time reading, and congrats on finishing the book until the very end.

If you're Gen Zer I'm sure you've learned lots regarding yourself. You've also learned about the options which are open to you and the ways you can grow to be the you that you wish to be. If you're the parent or guardian of Gen Zers I think that the book has opened your eyes to the differences between yourself and the Gen Zer , and how you can help Gen Zers excel.

Thank you and best of luck!

www.ingramcontent.com/pod-product-compliance
Lightning Source LLC
Chambersburg PA
CBHW050403120526
44590CB00015B/1809